A Sacred Identity: Practices for Awakening Consciousness

Allyson Kelley

Published by AKA Published, 2024.

A SACRED IDENTITY: PRACTICES FOR AWAKENING CONSCIOUSNESS

First edition. November 8, 2024.

Copyright © 2024 Allyson Kelley.

ISBN: 979-8991931014

Written by Allyson Kelley.

Endless dedication and thanks to the people who embrace
their sacred identities and show me how to live and heal.
Caitlin you are the best listener and practice of the
sacred--thank you for journeying with me on the back roads of
Central Oregon.

The spirit is the true self, not that physical figure which can be pointed out by your finger. — Marcus Tullius Cicero

Preface

C onsciousness in motion expresses itself as the objects of the universe in the eternal dance of life. – Deepak Chopra

Humankind is on the brink of the most significant spiritual crisis of our time. Many people do not have, or have lost, connection to their spirit. They are consumed with form, ego, and over-identification with social constructs and physical realities. This crisis is widespread, causing people to leave religion in droves, in search for God, the Divine, in them and in the world. This book counters the current paradigm and crisis through stories, research, and deep knowing with the Divine.

Key Points This Book Addresses:

There is a need to reframe and create a collective identity of wellbeing within our culture that is not based on race, ethnicity, income, or other socially constructed status.

People have lost their spiritual compass, the inner voice that is connected to God or the Divine.

How people see themselves and how they think other people see them can be helpful or harmful, depending on the mind's narrative or script.

Spirits don't have a social identity, an age, name, or label.

Identity impacts how you relate to the world around you. When you understand yourself and who you are, you can be more open and understanding of others.

Evidence of consciousness and awakening is measured in different ways, depending on what you believe and where you are on the path of life. Religion often divides rather than unites humanity - experiencing awakened consciousness from multiple ways of knowing and being can help you find spiritual grounding necessary to embody the love of God.

Collective Purpose

My purpose in writing this book is to lead readers onto a path of spiritual awakening rather than attachment to form-based identities. I believe it's possible at any age to live in a new way that is not obsessed with physical or form-based roles. It is possible for you to become grounded in the spiritual, Divine creation of the universe. This path is so essential because many people have lost their connection to God and to their sacred, spiritual selves. Some refuse to believe they are spiritual creatures having a human existence. No matter where you land on the continuum of non-spiritual to spiritual being, there is something in this book for you. The time you invest reading and reflecting in this book is worth the reward of tapping into your truest, fullest, spiritual powers as a spiritual being living in the current universe.

Why listen to me? These are questions that only you can answer.

> Why did you buy this book?

> Why do you want to spend time with the contents?

> Why should you listen to me?

I want you to know me and who I am. This feels vulnerable, it takes courage, and it pushes me outside of my comfort zone as I type from my picnic table at the end of a dirt road. I am not a public person. I am not someone who seeks attention or notoriety. But this is me as a socially constructed person with various form-based identities. You will get to know my spirit as you read this book. Because it is the spirit that is writing this book, it is not the professor, author, or researcher. My favorite spiritual gurus and mystics are people like Fr. Richard Rohr, Wayne Dyer, Eckart Tolle, Deepak Chopra, but I am not considered a spiritual guru or mystic by any stretch of the imagination. In fact, I might be the exact opposite. I have lived a full life of nearly 48 years, and in my life, I have experienced many physical and form-based identities. As a child who grew up in a lower middle-class home, we were considered low income. As a person who was sexually abused as a child, I have identified as a victim of sexual abuse. I am a mother, auntie, daughter, and friend. More recently, I identify as a doctoral trained researcher with a passion for social justice, health equity, and wellness. I proudly wear that egoic hat and form. As a Christian who believes in God and goes to church when life allows, I have belonged to religious groups and identified as one of them. I have been sober in mind, body, and from alcohol for three years. I will join a meeting and announce I am in recovery. I belong to these groups, sometimes as a writer and professor. I proudly identify with these titles. "What do you do?" Oh, I am a professor. I am an author. What is so very compelling about each of these identities is that they can connect us to one another, in a sameness kind of way. Because most of us are starving for connection and belonging (see the Surgeon General's report on epidemic loneliness and a suicide crisis in Chapter 1), we can see that social and form-based identities help us connect to others, find common ground, and at times, safe spaces to be who we are. However, the heart of who I am as a spiritual being is not connected to any of these experiences or socially constructed labels and identities. If you are still with me, and I hope that you are, this is the precise reason why I am somewhat qualified to write a book about the spiritual dimensions of wellness, walking with the Divine, and consciousness rising. I have been unwell, overidentified with various egoic forms and titles, and I have suffered because of it. Perhaps you have too. The beauty of these lived experiences is that because I have suffered, you may not need to, or at least not as much as I have. Some people tell me I am safe. I ground them. I have humor, perspective, a generous heart, and I can see the spiritual dimensions of wellbeing playing out in the lives of those around me, or the lack of spirit in some cases. You may have similar experiences or people who consider you a spiritually grounded person, a conscious human with a heart for God. This is perhaps the best label or identification that I can think of.

My Promise

After reading this book, I hope that when you are at a party and you have a thought stream through your conscious mind...like this person is not the same as me (Black, White, Gay, Straight, Poor, Rich, etc.) that you become the observer of this thought. Rather than acting out this thought with unconscious behaviors and unkind words, judgment, separateness, superiority, otherness, I want you to embrace the divine connection that you have with this physical person based on a sacred spiritual path. Perhaps this spirit showing up in physical form at a party is there to teach you something. You will encounter adverse experiences in your lifetime. If you have not, just wait, they will come. This book will give you practices and preparations that will strengthen your spirit so that when storms come, you can observe them, know them, and let them pass. Ultimately, my prayer is that all suffering ends in the world because people come to the realization that they are spiritual beings first, and that anything physical is just the spiritual world showing up in a form-based way. When you become spiritually grounded and centered, you pass these practices and deep knowledge on to others. They can see who you are at the spirit level, beyond the physical. Sharing your spirit with others allows you to find your ultimate purpose in life and your truest self. You will come to see the world as physical form-based structures as a representation of the spiritual realm. You will welcome everything that comes into your life and consciousness as something that can teach you how to grow and be your highest and best spiritual self. A Sacred Identity consists of six chapters. Chapters include lists, reflection prompts, scales, and practices to awaken your consciousness. I wrote these chapters in an order that makes sense to me, but the order may not make sense to you. Choose your path. As you read and absorb the content presented, take what benefits, and enriches your spirit, leave what does not. An Elder once told me that we get to decide what we take, and what we leave with (experiences, relationships, and knowing). This is powerful because ultimately you decide. You are the captain of your ship.

I am the captain of my ship. I am the master of my fate. The Divine is in us and with us.

Experiencing a Spiritual Life

I heard a story about a young man who was raised in a small village. Everyone in the village loved and adored him. It was a close community with everyone helping one another and raising the children of the village together. The boy got older and had a dream of traveling the world. He wanted to see places, experience things, and know what it meant to be an adventurer. He was gone for many years. In fact, he was gone for so long that people in the village forgot about him, some thought he had died. But one day he came back to the village. Everyone was so glad to see him. They wanted to hear all about his travels, his life, where he had been, and what he learned about the world, outside of this small village. They would gather up in the evenings after their work was completed and he would tell stories from his travels, the people he met, the rich culture, language, and the beauty of it all. One night the villagers said they wanted him to draw a map. Drawing a map would help them see all of the countries he had been to. So, several weeks passed and the boy, who was now a man, drew a map and shared it with the villagers. These are all of these places I have traveled to. The villagers looked at it in awe. They framed the map and hung it proudly on the village wall for everyone to see. They worshiped the map, in awe of the places and the freedom of this young man, their local villager. But it was not in the story or the map that the experiences happened. They could never truly tell what it was like to travel the world, because they were simply looking at a map, nothing more. To experience something and deeply know something, we have to walk on that road, be in those shoes, feel the air on our face, in those spaces of quietness, change, humility, love, adventure, and freedom. For some, they just have the map. That is where it ends. We can seek a spiritual life; we can go to church and read the Bible verses or meditate and practice silent retreats. But without a destination in mind, these are just maps. To truly know who we are as awakened spiritual beings, we must know where these maps are leading us. The key questions are.

What are your practices?

Where do you want them to lead you?

How do they lead you to experience a spiritual life?

Tell me about your life and practice so that I may understand you and you can understand me. This is all of the evidence that we need.

As we begin walking on the path to seek our true self, a higher level of consciousness, awakening, meaning, purpose, and happiness, we must be mindful and aware. The ego and various social identities can take over our thinking about our place and significance in this world as spiritual beings. Ego and thought will tell us who we are, who we are not, what we like, what we know, and who we belong to. These internal messages influence how we interact with others, our thoughts about those around us, and our behaviors. A key issue with social identities and the ego is that they often divide rather than unite us. The divisions of humankind are visible in every community, government, school system, family, faith-based organization, and country. Our children, young adults, and even older adults grow into the idea that separateness and otherness is the way to be. Everyone wants to feel unique, special, or different in some way. It is easy to get drawn into the values, ideals, dogmas, of socially constructed groups (income, race, professional affiliation, etc.) without deeply knowing who we are as spiritual beings and our connection to God or the Divine. Our emphasis on the physical rather than spiritual or formless is at the center of the spiritual crisis that we see in the world today.

You cannot tell me who I am, and I cannot tell you who you are. If you don't know your own identity. Who is going to identify you? - Thomas Merton

Going Deeper: Socially constructed identities and labels mask who we are as spiritual beings. We must be mindful, intentional, and aware of cultivating our spirit.

How we live is determined by what and how we think and what we do. It is normal to question our thoughts. But it is most important to remember that we are not our thoughts, we are the observer of the thoughts we have. As you begin reading this book a thought might arise like, "What is an awakened state of consciousness?" and "How is the current egoic crisis we are in related to spirituality?" We will answer these questions throughout this book. To begin with though, a spiritual being refers to something or someone that is not part of the physical or material formless world that we see. Sometimes the term spirit is used interchangeably with terms like soul, consciousness, or heart. A crisis is a time of intense difficulty, trouble, or danger. The absence of consciousness (unconsciousness) leads people into a state of crisis when challenges arise, they lack the ability to cope, self-regulate, ground themselves, and know that they are more than the physical form or anything that is happening to them in the present moment.

Michael Bernard Beckwith identified the following levels of spiritual development / awakening consciousness.[1] Which level of consciousness do you embody?

> Victim consciousness- Life is happening to me. I am affected by the world.

> Manifestor consciousness- Life is happening by me. I create life.

> Channel consciousness- Life is happening through me.

> One consciousness-Life is happening as me. I am one with God (called by many other names).

As you move through life, you may experience all of these states of consciousness, the goal, however, is one consciousness. There are signs that people are awakening to consciousness, they are being reborn, one with God, and aware of the Divine nature within them and the universe. At the same time, there are signs that a spiritual crisis is occurring, people are experiencing victim unconsciousness at multiple levels. They are asleep. A spiritual crisis is occurring in our world, evidence is everywhere that our eyes can see, and hearts can feel.

One of our problems today is that we are not well acquainted with the literature of the spirit. We are interested in the news of the day and the problems of the hour. – Joseph Campbell

Trigger warning. If you are feeling hopeless or in despair, please skip this section.

Gun violence is common. In 2021, more Americans died from gun-related injuries than any other time in history.

Discrimination and racism are commonly reported. Events like George Floyd's murder impacted how people think about racial inequality in the United States. Eight in ten Black Americans report they experienced discrimination because of their race or ethnicity.[2]

Sexual violence is common with 25% of men in the US reporting some form of contact sexual violence in their lifetime and one in three female victims experiencing rape for the first time between the ages of 11 and 17.[3]

Drug and alcohol addiction are on the rise. More than 932,000 people have died from overdoses in the US since 1999. Opioids are driving the crisis, with 75% of all deaths in 2020 were caused by opioids.[4]

Suicide is a permanent decision to temporary problem. Suicide is a leading cause of death in the US. In 2021, 48,183 people died by suicide in the United States, that is 1 death every 11 minutes.[5]

Poverty impacts more than 40% of the world's population, policies, and programs designed to address the material poverty crisis are not working.[6] Poverty divides and excludes people and populations rather than connecting and supporting them as spiritual beings. When basic needs are not met, it is difficult for people to consider their spiritual wellbeing.

Disconnection impacts every facet of our wellbeing leading to pervasive physical, mental, and social conditions. Caused by loneliness and isolation, when people are disconnected, they are more likely to use drugs, alcohol and die prematurely.[7]

Social media impacts every aspect of how most Americans live. People spend more time on their smartphones and less time developing healthy relationships with fellow humans, in-person. New research shows that poor mental health, depression, and suicide are related to increased time on social media and smartphones, teen girls are among the most vulnerable groups. Social media creates a false sense of connection and friendship, spreads misinformation and disinformation, and creates a distorted reality of the world. Because social media alters cognitive and brain development in youth and adults, it is considered a significant public health crisis.

Loss of faith is happening at unprecedented rates. Americans are leaving their religious houses and groups in record numbers. While some people have found God and spiritual connections in organized religions, others have not. In fact, many have had the opposite experiences, leaving the churches due to sexual abuse, hypocrisy, and politics. A Pew Research Center study reports that 65% of American adults describe themselves as Christians when asked to describe their faith, this is down 12% from what it was ten years ago.[8] People are leaving religion; it has failed to remind them of their Divine nature and sacredness. These examples are outward signs of an internal crisis of the spirit. But I rarely see news headlines or research that calls attention to the crisis of the spirit. Do you?

When you're experiencing a crisis as an individual, that's what St. John of the Cross calls "the dark night of the soul." You're wrestling with God. You're doing what you need to do to handle what's coming up out of you that you don't understand. It's personal. You're getting a divorce; your child is ill ... or you're just having the catastrophe of everyday life. – Barbara Holmes

These outward signs of crisis are wrong, and they need to be made right. Nobody wants to experience gun violence or even commit gun violence or abuse, but it happens. When you look around you, what evidence do you see that a spiritual crisis is occurring among human beings on this Earth? Have you stopped to notice what is happening?

Have you asked yourself, "Why is gun violence increasing?" When you begin to ask these questions, you cannot help but look within. Events happening in the physical universe are a direct reflection of where people are spiritually, mentally, and emotionally.

Where have we gone astray?

How did we get so far away from our truest and highest selves to allow these crises to occur as we stand unconsciousness, hopeless, numb, detached, and angry?

What is causing such spiritual suffering?

Events like suicide cause tremendous suffering for the survivors. There is much to learn about how we respond when tragedy and trauma occurs. Instead of numbing the mind and spirit with drugs, food, or other addictive behaviors, we can choose a different path. We can sit silently and be grateful for the loved one and the life that they shared with us. We can be still, without judgment knowing that they are no longer suffering. I realize this is easier said than done.

Being spiritual has nothing to do with what you believe and everything to do with your state of consciousness. - Eckhart Tolle

Spiritual Awakening Checklist

Spiritual awakening depends on your worldview and cannot be generalized to all people, beliefs, and ideas about what it means to be spiritually well. When you look around the world or your world, do you see God? Where is the Great Universal Spirit living and being? Is it in the eyes of people, the actions and love of others, the wisdom and offerings given to you by elders and people who care for you? The main challenge with developing a spiritual awakening checklist is that it uses form-based models and requires thinking to assess where one is at on the continuum of being spiritually awakened. Phil Friedman developed a series of helpful scales, including the Spiritual Awakening Scale.[9] Answer the questions based on a response of '0' "not at all" to '5' "a great deal".

Spiritual Awakening Scale

I am aware of my true nature.

I know that awareness is everywhere, not just in me.

I live for uplifting the whole.

I place maintaining my spirituality as a high priority for me.

I understand my life's purpose through my spirituality.

I receive a great deal of fulfillment from my spirituality.

I am clear about my next step, my next inspired action.

I align with my high power/intelligence to contribute to others.

I am aware of awareness itself.

I see space around everything.

I am able to include everything within me, to let everything in.

I am perfect just as I am.

I am able to let go of any investment in the future.

I am perfect where I am.

I have lots of compassion, empathy, integrity, and love.

I easily create partnerships with others.

I am able to do little things with great love.

Higher scores indicate a greater level of spiritual awakening where lower scores may indicate awakening is not part of your awareness. Friedman[9] collected data with this scale from 563 people, their average score was 54.72.

What is your score?

How does your spiritual awakening score compare to others?

Our spirit or the Divine does not have a form. It is separate from the mind or the physical universe, which includes the body. Our spirit does not age. Everything we can sense in the physical world was once known as an unmanifested spiritual source. More importantly, form-based identities and labels given to certain groups of people based on their race, class, gender, sexual orientation, profession, socioeconomic status, religious affiliation, and more, have very little to do with our spirit.

Explain what your spirit is in words.

Draw your spirit on a piece of paper.

Capture your spirit in a photograph.

Reflections for Going Deeper

Read. What did you read that speaks to your spirit?

Reflect. In what ways might you use these words to become more spiritually awakened?

Remember. What can you remember about who you are as a conscious spiritual being?

Abide. What do you accept?

1 Who Are you?

Those who are awake live in a constant state of amazement. - Buddha

Who are you? Why are you here? If this book has landed in your lap, then you might already be thinking about the burning question that most of us have at some point in our lives. Who am I? Why am I here? How did I get here and where to go when leaving this Earth? It would be easy to answer these questions based on our Earthly identities and physical forms. My name is .... I am here because someone gave birth to me. Obviously, we could go deeper with these questions. Like, what is the purpose of human suffering? If there is a God or Creator of the universe, why do bad things happen to good people? We could go on for a while about the Why's of existence. Or we could stop and consider that the very thinking about who we are and why we are here is part of a spiritual dimension that, if uncovered, can bring us to a place of peace, connection, and assurance that we are living and breathing on the path that is meant for us. We must consider our view of the world and how others view the world, so that we can enter into a spiritual realm. The challenge we face as a society, a collective group of humans, is not material; it is not based on material deprivation, climate change, politics, violence, or poverty. The challenge is a spiritual one. When I use the term spiritual, I mean not of material form. Spirituality is concerned with the human spirit (soul) rather than the material and physical things we experience. Much of our individual and collective efforts as a society have been focused in the wrong direction—on physical and material things. Writing this book might be all wrong. Am I to sit and contemplate spiritual principles and awakening when such unconsciousness leads to suffering, injustice, violence, poverty, discrimination, and racism? And what am I to do with the privilege I inherently possess as a white female with a doctoral degree and time to write? These are contemplative questions, but one of the practices I have not fully mastered is the art of contemplative acts. I am not, by nature, contemplative. I am energetic and reactive and like to do, act, and feel alive in the physical world. Laughter and nature are my go-to spiritual medicines.

What do you spend time thinking about?

Why are you here?

What are your spiritual medicines?

Research, Worldviews and the Path

You are on the path to knowing who you are. I know parts of who I am, at least how the external world sees who I am. Our identities and perspectives determine our worldview. I am a professor and researcher, recovering, and undoing these identities. When I was completing my doctoral studies, I learned about positionality, paradigms, and philosophical worldviews. Believe it or not, I had not really thought much about worldview before that time; I was busy trying to survive. As a student and researcher, worldview comes into play early in our academic training because it outlines our assumptions and beliefs about the things we research. We were taught early in our academic studies that researchers must be forthcoming with their worldview because it drives their selection of research methods, analysis, and dissemination. Worldviews also can be checked and reviewed for bias and validity. There are multiple philosophical worldviews, but I was taught about these four: post-positivism, constructivism, transformative, and pragmatism. As a researcher, there are times we are expected to write about our religion and experience in relation to the data and population we are working with. For example, as an individual with the lived experience of recovery from substance use, I state that if I am writing or researching this topic. It gives me credibility and influences my positionality, paradigm, and worldview. If you want to know more about these worldviews, read a book or search the world wide web. I am not an expert on worldviews, and this book is not about worldviews or research positions, but worldviews can help you make sense of how and why experiences happen, ways in which theories and evidence are created to explain wellness and spirituality, and more. We can all be researchers in our own right, even without the advanced training or degrees.

I have researched the spiritual dimensions of wellbeing for nearly two decades. My reasons for researching spiritual dimensions of wellbeing are not just academic endeavors; they are personal. I was sitting with a friend at a VRBO in Lander, Wyoming talking about this book and my struggles with writing about the spiritual dimensions of wellness. She happens to be a treatment program director and wise tribal Elder with long white hair, beautiful skin, and a wit that is quicker than most. I told her, "We write books (if we are privileged in that way) because we want to fully understand something." Leading up to writing this book, I did not fully understand how my view of the world and spirituality make up the whole of who I am as a spiritual being. She chuckled and gazed passed my eyes for a long while, not blinking, and said, "Of course that is why you write these books." She knew this about me all along. I did not. If you are like me, you might want to know how to be spiritually well. For me, this curiosity and seeking are part of my daily practice, prayer, and work. My philosophical worldview guiding this writing is both constructivist and transformative. From a constructivist view, I seek understanding. I am approaching the concept of spiritual wellbeing based on social, historical, and spiritual experiences. Because I am writing based on my experiences and the experiences of others, I value multiple positions, identities, and views about the spiritual dimensions of wellbeing throughout the life course. I also embrace a transformative worldview that recognizes power and justice, political and dualistic views, and a focus on positive growth. While this is not a book about research, it is essential to recognize that scientific knowledge, beliefs, dogmas, theologies, and teachings are primarily influenced by the positionality of the researcher, the scientist, the policy maker, or other people with power. Because I am a researcher, I have been influenced in this way. My spirit has been touched by these bodies of research, this way of deep knowing, and it shows up in nearly everything that I do. But at the end of the day, my research and worldviews do not impress the Divine. The Divine loves me and cherishes me, without asking anything in return.

And so, I tell you, keep on asking, and you will receive what you ask for. Keep on seeking, and you will find. Keep on knocking, and the door will be opened to you. For everyone who asks, receives. Everyone who seeks, finds. And to everyone who knocks, the door will be opened. - Jesus of Nazareth

Going Deeper: Our positions matter because they sway what we think and know. There is a bias and subjectivity wrapped up in these positions, egoic forms needing to be right. It's easier to belong to a group of form-based identities rather than stand alone. But the spiritual path is a deeply personal one, it's your road to take and yours alone. I can tell you my journey, I will do this over the next several chapters. But this journey will not be yours. My ways are not your ways, and my knowing is not yours. Part of developing your own worldviews and finding your path is recognizing what makes you uniquely you, different from the 5 billion other physical humans showing up with form-based identities in the world.

Identities

Personal and social identities create the whole of who we are as human beings and our spiritual experiences, contributing to or taking away from our wellbeing. Both identities come from our experiences with others and the world around us. Identities can be both fixed and dynamic. For example, I was born as a female at birth. I was a baby, then a child, a teen, a young adult, adult, and now I am moving toward the second half of my life. Eventually, I will be an old woman. Throughout my life, my gender identity as a female has not changed, but what it means to be a female has. If my life was unfolding in the 1950s, my role as a female would be limited to certain professions, nursing, secretary, stay-at-home mom, or teacher. I would likely exist in a traditional marriage with a husband who works and controls the house budget, vacations, decisions, discipline, and children. It is 2024; I am a mother and care for my elder mom, but this is where the traditional role as a female in US society ends. I've been married twice for 28 of the 48 years I have lived, both times to older men who were probably not a good fit for me. I remain married to my second husband, although we live in separate cities most of the time. I manage my own house, children, budget, and decisions. I have different experiences as a cis-gender female living today, and the world has varied expectations of me. But being a female is not the most essential identity that I embrace. My soul is what is most important; the essence of who I am without this physical shell that I inhabit. At the core of our personal and social identities is the soul. Later in this book, we will explore the soul in relation to our identity and worldview, but for now, stay with the idea that you are a soul. Living in a body and cultivating your soul identity is the most important life work you can undertake.

I am a professor, so I like to talk about my teaching experiences and what I learn from students. The spring 2023 semester just ended at the university. I tell my daughter I need a break every semester when I am nearing the end. I need to take a semester off. But after a few days pass, I miss my students, the content, the challenge, and the possibilities of impacting the lives of future leaders, parents, and visionaries. Over the years, I have noticed that self-concept and self-identity significantly predict how students perform, interact, and succeed in my classes. I ask students to complete an assignment during the first week of classes because I want to know who they think they are and who they identify with. This exercise also tells me much about their willingness to be vulnerable with a professor they do not know and may not like or trust.

This is how the assignment goes in my undergraduate race, ethnicity, and health class. You can complete this now if you want.

What is your name?

The first time I noticed a racial difference was....

What is the current racial landscape of your world - at home, work, school, and social activities?

Next, I asked them about the Big 8 Social Identities. Some students are unfamiliar with how race differs from ethnicity or what nationality and ability identity mean. The terms below help students formulate ideas about who they are as form-based identities and give insight into their spiritual nature. The social identities often relate to a student's level of spirituality and spiritual practices. If we are to truly understand and know who we are, as spiritual beings we must consider these social identities and observe how other people embrace these identities as well. This is what I tell my students about the Big 8 Social Identities and what we know from the research about identities and spirituality/wellness.

Racial identity shapes privileged status for some and undermines the social standing of others. Race identifies a group that is socially defined but based on physical criteria, such as skin color and facial features. White people in America are losing their majority status; in 2021, just 59% of the US population was white.[10] The multiracial population in the US increased 276% from 2010 to 2020 and continues to grow.[11] Researchers explored the racial identity of Black Americans and found that their cultural values and practices increase their health and wellbeing. Black racial identity was associated with increased spirituality. [12] Ethnicity identity is defined by culture, language, and country of origin. This relates to a person or to a large group of people who share a national, cultural, and/or linguistic heritage, whether or not they reside in their countries of origin. Hispanics and Latino Americans are the largest ethnic group in the US. A national study of Latino Americans found that most identify as Catholic, and the longer they have been in the US (enculturated), the more likely they are to utilize prayer for healing and mind-body therapies. [13] Sexual orientation identity is defined as an emotional, romantic, sexual, spiritual, affectional, and/or relational attraction to another person or persons. Self-labels might include gay, lesbian, heterosexual, same gender loving, bisexual, pansexual, queer, or straight. A national poll on sexual orientation shows changes in status based on age. For example, 6% of millennials born between 1981 and 1996 reported they were bi-sexual; this increased to 15% among generation G born between 1997 and 2003. [14] A paper published in the American Psychological Association journal reported that sexual minorities feel that spirituality makes them feel worse about their sexual orientation, and spirituality was associated with heteronormativity. [15] Gender identity is how a person sees themselves, for example: as a woman, as a man, as a transgender/genderqueer person, as a combination, or as none of these categories. This can be a person's masculine, feminine, or other gendered sense. Gender identity is also changing based on age; 1% of millennials identified as transgender, and 2% of Generation Z.[15] An article by Fr. Richard Rohr in the Huffington Post explores the role of gender, God, and spirituality. We may have different ways find spirituality based on our gender identity, but the end goal is the same:

being guided by One who is neither male nor female.[16] Ability identity is the physical or mental capacity to do something or perform successfully. Able-bodied individuals do not suffer developmental, psychological, learning, physical, or illiteracy disabilities. About 13% of the US population experience a disability, which is more common among older people.[17] Studies of spirituality among people with disabilities have found that people with hearing, physical, and emotional disability are more likely to pray several times a day and have a turning point when they become less committed to a relationship and more committed to a spiritual way of life.[18] Religion/Spirituality identity is an institutionalized or personal system of beliefs and practices related to the divine. A recent poll by the Pew Research Center showed that about 63% of the US population self-identify as Christian; this is down from 75% a decade ago. Among these, 40% are protestant, and 21% are catholic. And just 45% of adults pray daily, down from 58% in 2007.[19] Nationality identity is the identifier expressed by the individual's country of origin. About 80% of Americans descended from Europe. What it means to be an American has changed over time. Pew Research reports that while ideological divides persist regarding national pride, traditions, practices, and discrimination, the US and Western European countries are becoming more inclusive, which relates to connection and spirituality.[20] Socioeconomic status identity is the social standing based on income and/or one's position in society (working poor, working class, middle class, and upper class). We know that people who experience poverty and low income have high religious beliefs but not spiritual ones. One of my good friends who lives on the Northern Cheyenne Reservation in Montana told me that being poor means not having any relatives.

In my Spring 2023 semester, 26 students completed the exercise. This is what I found. Most students identified as Black. Ethnic identity varied from Hispanic, Indian, and Ethiopian. Most were heterosexual. Many were working class or working poor. Religion and spiritual identity included Christian, Catholic, Muslim, or none. As we moved through class, I saw identities shifting. For example, students who started the class identifying as Black or African American might reflect and learn that they are only Black American because their ancestors do not originate from Africa. This has also happened with American Indian students who embraced their tribal affiliations throughout the course after learning about the Indigenous peoples of the US.

I have learned that social identities are not always what they seem. While this exercise focuses on racial identities and health, you can easily see how these identities shape our worldview and thoughts about who we are and why we are here. Here are some examples from my students and my work over the years.

Gangs and chains. Many years ago, I worked with a sociologist who talked about the protective benefits of being in a gang. She had worked in Los Angeles with some of the most extreme gangs, violence, trauma, and identity presence. Young kids join gangs because they had no other choice. They soon learned the benefits of being in a gang, from friends, stability, housing, kinship, and even drug access. There was an identity and affiliation with gangs that were not part of their normal lives. Studies show gangs provide members with a sense of belonging, connection, and mattering that they have not received from other relationships or experiences in their lives. While this might be difficult for some to grasp, the main point here is that not every identity can be viewed dualistically–good or bad, right or wrong.

Personal and social identities also relate to a person's spiritual wellbeing. Sometimes identification with an undesirable persona or deficit perpetuates it. What we tell ourselves about who we are and what we are capable of is driven by the stories we tell ourselves. Here is an example.

John is a peer recovery support specialist. This means he has lived experience of addiction and has recovered or been sober for two years. John shows up at every meeting and tells the group he is an alcoholic (or he experiences alcohol use disorder). Although he is in recovery, John talks about his relationship problems, time in jail for domestic violence, and failed suicide attempts. All of this relates back to his addiction to alcohol. John cannot step away from this narrative and social identity. Every time he retells his story, he relives his time in prison, failed relationships, and time spent in the psychiatric ward. At some point, John will need to create a new personal and social identity that is not tied to these stories. Mainly because every time he tells the story, he goes back in time, and he is not living in the present. He is living in the past. His old identity is not serving him any longer.

Going Deeper: Our worldview is not just how we see the world. Our worldview is being aware of how we experience the world, react to things happening around us, feel emotions and connections, and live out our daily lives. Worldview guides our position as humans, creates our identity, and implicitly creates our entire life experience.

Who do you say you are?

Now that you know who I am, who are you? If you are traveling on a plane, making small talk at your son's soccer game and the person next to you asks, "What do you do?" You probably politely respond with a job-related answer. I am a teacher. I am in law enforcement. I am a lawyer. I am .... The identification with labels and physical titles is infinite. Have you ever thought about what would happen if someone asked, "Who are you?" Would you respond, "I am Sam's dad?" Or would you say, "I am a spirit showing up in a human costume, here on this Earth for a very short time, to do sacred work." If you try this second response, be aware that you might be labeled a freak, mystic, or someone who is completely out of touch with reality. Although I would add, this response is the most in-touch with reality of the conscious form.

Conditioned Mind and Our Environment

Our minds create scripts about who we are and who other people think we are. But you are not your mind or your ego. The conditioned mind is constantly challenging our identity, who we think we are, and who we want the world to think we are. Think back to your earliest memory.

What was happening in your environment?

How old were you?

What did you see? Feel? Hear? Experience?

Depending on what you remember and your experience, this time and memory shaped your interpretation of the world today and every thought that you have.

Who was the person that was there?

Was that you?

What part of you was in that experience?

Your physical body, as it is today, is likely not there. Your mind was there, much like it is today. Your spirit was likely aware of the experience. This is important since we know that our mind is conditioned and programmed at an early age to see and view things according to our environment, social conditions, and family values. Over time our minds are conditioned to create a false self or ego. The false self is not who we indeed are. Our egoic mind tells us we need to fit into a world driven by winning, money, beauty, fame, recognition, and status. Left unaware of their ego, many people live out their lives constantly thinking, seeking, feeling, discontent and disrupted.

Early in my teaching career I taught environmental public health at a small college in Billings, Montana. We worked with tribal colleges on four reservations in Montana. This was one of my first times considering the impact of environment and conditions on wellness. Trauma was pervasive in these communities and in the lives of my students. Extreme poverty, colonization, discrimination, poor educational systems, sexual abuse, violence, addiction, substandard housing, and more. The conditions simply did not promote physical or spiritual wellness. Multiple studies on animals and now humans demonstrate what happens to the mind and body at an early age when they are exposed to trauma or adverse childhood events. These events range from being physically or sexually abused to having a family member in prison. In Bruce Perry's book, The Boy Who Was Raised by a Dog, the importance of the environment and conditions on the mind becomes very clear. Drawing from the field of developmental psychology and his clinical work, this book explains what happens to the brain when children are exposed to extreme stress and trauma. In one case, a boy was neglected and raised by his dog. The child is left hopeless when the dog dies, and his family falls apart. Other historical accounts of humans being raised by wolves, dogs, chickens, monkeys, and other animals demonstrate what happens when children grow up with limited human encounters. The story of a boy named Mthiyane speaks to this. He was five when he was found living with a group of monkeys in South Africa. Although he spent just one year (age 4 to 5) with monkeys, he still could not talk at age 17. He walked and jumped like a monkey. He could not speak or socialize with other children. While these are extreme conditions, they make a point. Our interpretation of the world, the thoughts our mind tells us about what is accurate and true, come from our early childhood or formative years.

As adults, these thoughts become how we make sense of the world. How we assign meaning and value to certain things, and how to live. The labels we place on things are part of the ego, and our way of making sense of what is happening to us, both good, bad, and neutral. My dog is a dog. She does not know that she is called a dog. She just knows she is who she is, second by second.

The Divine and Worldviews

Worldviews are a collection of stories, values, ideas, attitudes, and beliefs about the world and everything and being in the world. Most worldviews are implicit, meaning we experience them without knowing or intentionally practicing them. Worldviews are found in individuals, families, communities, cultures, and institutions. Entire books have been written on the topic of worldviews. If you are not sure what worldview you embrace, there are many books mentioned in this section that you could check out at your local library or search the world wide web. There are many good-hearted people in the world who are not spiritual. They follow the dogma, "If you cannot measure it, it does not exist." Consider your worldview today.

Where did your worldview come from?

Has it changed over time?

If you are not sure what your worldview is, consider what you value. Also, consider what you believe; what do you know to be true? This is a start. Not all worldviews embrace the belief and knowing that there is a transcendent and spiritual dimension of reality that connects us to our deepest purpose and meaning. There are three basic worldviews about gods, God, or the Divine that most humans can be classified into when it comes to belief.

Secular Humanism/Atheism/Atheists - There are not gods, God, or the Divine.

Pantheism/Panentheist - The belief that God is in everything and everyone.

Monotheism - The belief in one God.

Secular humanism is a non-religious worldview based on science, nature, and ethics. Here, people create their own ideas about morality. There is no faith, dogma, doctrine, or mystical explanation of reality. Rather humanistic worldviews promote fairness, equity, responsibility, and respect. The secular worldview denies a God-centered spiritual dimension. This can be problematic when developing a spiritual foundation and identity.

I have also encountered students and families who are agnostic and atheistic. These are slightly different identities, where atheists believe in no god(s) and agnostics are not sure if there is a god. While they have no foundational beliefs in God, they believe in service. Here is an example of an agnostic worldview. When we first moved to central Oregon, I made it a point to continue serving in a food kitchen similar to what we did with our church in New Mexico. We quickly found the Family Kitchen, a place in downtown Bend that served daily meals to the homeless, indigent, and hungry. My daughter Caitlin and I showed up on Sundays to work our 4.5-hour shift. There was a family that volunteered with us. While I never asked them, from our interactions and conversations I assumed they embraced an agnostic worldview. They were not Christian. They did not believe in God. But they did believe in service.

We know that spiritual practice and belief in a higher power help us through times of crisis and despair, but what about people who have no spiritual foundation? Cognitive scientists conducted an online survey of participants throughout the world with a focus on secular worldviews. They asked atheists about coping, and most mentioned belief in the scientific method, rejecting beliefs that are not grounded in evidence, and living life to the fullest.[21] Atheists do not need the Divine to live a full life. They are still searching for the scientific evidence of the Divine.

Here is a story of an atheist I know…

Jane is a juvenile district court judge. She wears no makeup and has a few tattoos and piercings in places I would not. She wears Carhartt overalls and jeans and always a vest. Her hair is short, curly, and always clean. I got to know Jane doing some volunteer work in our community. She and I have different worldviews, but we are united in that we think volunteering is part of what makes us human and our community a better place. Jane has a heart for justice. She walks for justice, looks like justice, and makes sure that she does everything in her power to promote fairness, responsibility, and integrity. While she has tolerance for other worldviews, she is married and deeply entrenched in her own. This is not a bad thing, and it's not a judgment of Jane. It is just the dimension of time and space that she occupies. Her thoughts about who she wants to be are based on these principles. Recently, while she was volunteering, there were some kids who did not pick up a chess set they were using. Recently, there were some kids who did not pick up the chess set. She approached them and asked them to pick it up. They laughed at her and left. She followed them and asked again. They came back and partially picked up the chess set. At the same time, they were looking her up and down, staring in places they should not. I asked her how she felt about this a few weeks later. She said it still bothered her that the kids would be this disrespectful, and there was nothing that she could do to change their behaviors. Here the secular humanistic worldview that promotes responsibility and respect failed. These kids were not yet there.

Fr. Richard Rohr is a Franciscan priest and bestselling author. His book the Universal Christ is among the best I have read. And, after reading this book I felt that Rohr was definitely a pantheist. But he is not. He prefers the term Panentheist, which means that God is in everything. He does not believe that all is god in the universe we find ourselves in. His teachings stress the divine nature of the universe and the sacredness of life and mysticism.

My work with Indigenous communities has given me new ideas about where God is, who God is, and what spirituality looks like in everyday practice. Many call this pantheism. Some Indigenous people use the Medicine Wheel, where everything is interconnected and balanced. The wheel is a circle with four quadrants that represent four directions, four winds, four seasons, four stages of life, and four areas of wellness. Recovery centers use the Medicine Wheel to explore balance and wellbeing in people recovery. The first step in healing is to find the Creator. Where is the Creator in the world, in self, in relationships, and in elders and wisdom. A young man was referred to an outpatient treatment center for recovery support. The recovery center uses the Medicine Wheel and 12 step program from White Bison. He completed a worksheet with the Medicine Wheel and reflected on each of the areas. His first task was to find the creator, then himself. This process took a while. He did not see the Creator in his addiction, the abuse he endured throughout his childhood, or the racist comments that people made to him in the local Walmart store. His journey to finding the Creator was to see that the Creator is in everything and everyone. The Medicine Wheel is a visual depiction of the interconnectedness of all life and experiences. It has been a few years. He is working is recovery plan. He is attending spiritual activities at the recovery center. Creator is in him, and he is in Creator. Life is balancing out for him. Soon he will become an elder. This wisdom and experience will be passed down to future generations.

Christian Worldview

The Christian or biblical worldview embraces the teachings that God created the heavens and the Earth 6,000 years ago, and that Christ is the Son of God. The teachings found in the Bible show people how to live. The ten commandments are one of the guideposts from the Bible that many use as they develop perspectives about what it means to be grounded in a Christian worldview. Commandments are a reminder that the world does not revolve around us. Here are the abbreviated ten commandments in case you are not familiar with them from Exodus 20:17.You shall have no other gods before God. You shall not make idols. You shall not take the name of the Lord God in vain. Remember the sabbath and keep it holy. Honor your father and mother. You shall not murder. You shall not commit adultery. You shall not steal. You shall not bear false witness against your neighbor. You shall not covet.

Here are some stories of a Christian/Monotheist families I know...

The Smiths have five kids between the ages of 6 and 17. They live in a barn on 40 acres outside of a small town in Oregon. Mrs. Smith homeschools her children. Mr. Smith is an EMT. They are what I would call conservative Christians. They are opposed to abortion, divorce, working on Sundays, and any activity they view as immoral (there is a long list). They serve in their church and in community, and they are somewhat righteous. I asked Mrs. Smith recently about inviting some Mormons and Jehovah Witnesses to a community gathering. The gathering intended to bring youth in from all denominations to know Jesus. Mrs. Smith said, "No, we cannot invite those kids, there are too many dogmatic differences in what we believe and what they believe." I immediately felt the division that many experience when leaving the church, dropping a religion, or being chastised for religious expression and beliefs. The Smith family continues to live out their daily lives, mostly asleep. Another Christian family I know is loving, generous, kindhearted, and inclusive. They've adopted three of their four children. They love like nobody else. They attend a community church when life allows. They find God in service, nature, and being. These are the kinds of Christians that the world needs more of. They are Christ like, not religious. They are awake. I think they have found the Divine.

Spiritual Worldview: I am a spirit, I have a body

People who embrace a spiritual worldview do life a bit differently. While they may embrace multiple social and philosophical worldviews, their spirit is at the center of every experience they have, every thought that comes from their mind, every observation, every choice they make. They may identify with being agnostic, atheist, monotheist, or pantheist/panentheist. The spiritual worldview is based on the belief that there is more to our existence than just what we see and feel. While we are spiritual beings all of the time, sometimes my mind and body forget. I say things I do not want to say. I do things that are embarrassing, offensive, and not spiritually connected to my highest good. It is with this understanding and acceptance that I see my spiritual worldview unfolding. It is not the only worldview I possess, and it is not always the most dominant, but it is there. Human development literature tells us that our worldview begins to take shape between the ages of one and three years old. Worldviews may change over the life course based on what we feel is good, right, and just. Over the years, there have been teachers, gurus, Elders, pastors, priests, and prophets who have promoted the spiritual worldview in my life and in the lives of others. Here are some examples of those people and how they have influenced my rising consciousness as a spirit connected to the Divine who lives in everything and everyone.

Here are some stories of people who embrace the spiritual worldview.

John was a psychology professor who spent his time and thought on the philosophies of religion, dogmas, New Age thinking, ceremonies, and spiritual practices. He embraced the spiritual worldview that all things emanate from a universal God. John could not communicate with others, he had few friends, and students felt he was unreachable, out in the left field, and not grounded in the physical reality of life. John retired from the university early and became a recluse. He is awake, just not in the world. Joe is one pastor I will not forget. He is small in stature but grand in spirit. With a Ph.D. in Theology from Duke, he could tell stories, recite scripture, and teach the Bible like no other. Joe taught about the spiritual worldview using teachings from the Methodist church. His spiritual teachings were backed by the church and opportunities for the religious to show up and act out their faith and beliefs. Some got to spirituality; others did not. But the goal here was that he introduced people to these teachings in a humble, kind, and magical way. His goal was not religion, it was introducing people to the loving Divine Creator of the Universe. Eckhart Tolle is perhaps one of the greatest thinkers and speakers on spirituality and worldview. Reading his book Stillness Speaks begins an awakening in the human soul and sparks an awareness that reminds us we are much more than our physical body, our thoughts, and our ego. Fr. Fr. Richard Rohr is a mystic, philosopher, and Franciscan priest. He stresses the spiritual worldview from a biblical and historical perspective. Richard's teachings are found in dozens of books and podcasts. His book, Breathing Underwater, lays out the 12-step process of recovery and how it mirrors biblical teachings and principles. The first time I read this book, it changed what I thought about my own spirituality, recovery, and the Bible. What I find most intriguing about his approach to the spiritual worldview is that he stresses that nothing stands alone. Rather than approach spiritual worldviews from a dualistic perspective (i.e., right, and wrong), he embraces all spiritual worldviews as sacred, similar, and united in their teachings to bring awareness and awakening to the human race. Susan is a Mandan Hidatsa elder, mother, and grandparent. She is not famous by social media or Hollywood standards, but she is perhaps one of the biggest thinkers on spiritual worldviews, teachings, and beings. I first met Susan in 2005. We were working together, and at the time, I did not understand her. She was quiet. Sometimes her head was completely down during meetings. She was, in a sense, part of a different dimension. I did not know at that time that she was practicing her spiritual worldview. She was praying, she was listening, and she was present. She just showed up in different ways. There are many others who embody spiritual worldviews and who have influenced the writing of this book and how I show up in writing today. Their teachings and spirit are infused throughout this book.

Who are the spiritual teachers in your life?

What is it about how they live that makes them embrace a spiritual worldview and dimension of wellness?

Materialistic Worldview: What you see is what you get.

I have encountered humans in my lifetime who have not experienced anything spiritual. They are overly concerned with the material and physical world. We can learn about worldview by simply observing the cars people drive, where they live, what they wear, and what they spend their time, money, and energy on. It is not a secret. Those with a materialistic worldview believe that reality is made up of that which is visible, created, produced, and tangible. In the US and other industrialized nations, consumerism is the anchor of a materialistic worldview. I was visiting with a colleague yesterday on Zoom. Bundled up in a ski jacket, she said, "You need to wear some long johns or turn up the heat." I told her I could bear the cold, "I am from Alaska and Montana. This is nothing." From there, we talked about why I chose to stand in a freezing cold office rather than turn on the heat. I have the heat, and I could even pay for the heating bill, but that was not the point. The point was that I am a saver. I don't want to spend money if I don't need to. And this goes back to my childhood of not having enough. In some ways, I have a materialistic view of the world because I place value on things that are material that money can buy, like heat. While my spirit resists the thought of being materialistic in any way, my conditioned mind and ego tell me I need more, I will never have enough, and I need to save. These are all the wrong messages. I need to work on reprogramming the narrative of not having enough. Families here in Oregon have money. Families are also living in poverty and middle class. Ruby Payne developed a framework for understanding generational poverty as a culture that most of her students have in common. Within a culture of poverty, money is viewed as something to be shared with others. In contrast, wealthy people view money as something that should be invested, and middle-class people view money as something that should be managed. Poor people are concerned about food access and quantity. Middle-class people want to like the food they eat. Wealthy people want the food to be presented in an aesthetically pleasing manner. From these examples, you can see the way that our culture conditions our minds to act in specific ways around scarcity or abundance.

Here are more stories of the materialistic worldview from my own life.

Every 4th of July, our tiny airport opens its runway for drag racing. Cars line up on the takeoff line and speed down the runway faster than I would like to go on any given day. I went last year. Some of the cars were shiny, new, and nice. Others were barely hanging on with mufflers dragging, driven by young kids with cowboy hats living their biggest dream. I was thinking about those cars and the people that drive them. Do they just drive these for racing, or do the cars get them from one stop to the next? As I watch, I listen in on a conversation about the drag race among wealthy people… "Yeah, I think I will just buy a car for that race. A new car. Fast one. Why not? The other wealthy person responded, "Wow, that's impressive." The conditioned mind, materialistic worldviews, and ego are all woven into this conversation. Can you see it and feel it? A new car will tell the world I have money, status, privilege, and material wealth. The fastest car wins the race. I will win. This is what the ego wants, to win the race and impress the masses. The problem with the race is that it is over in the afternoon; the thrill is fleeting The winners with their new cars, purchased just for the race, no longer satisfy the ego or conditioned mind. The thoughts about racing become distant. The ego searches for meaning in a new race, a new car, a new drug… or anything else the mind tells it that it needs to be worthy and enough. Tom is in his 70s. He sold tractors for a major company and retired in his 50s. He married a wealthy English woman, and they settled right next to one of my family members. I visit often, so over the years, I have come to know Tom and his story. Tom talks non-stop about money, material goods, material experiences, real estate, and travel. Although he is in his 70s, he still values and talks about these things, almost to the point of obsession. He wants to know who in the neighborhood has the most money. How many properties they own. The types of cars they drive. The vacations they take. The type of champagne they buy. The list goes on. I thought that Tom would change over the years, but his materialist worldview has not. Last night, Tom asked how I was doing. I am great. Never better. Oh yeah. Skiing has been wonderful this year. I cannot believe it. John owns 15 acres on Kauai in Princeville. "Have you been there?" He asks this a few times. I nod yes. I have been there to reassure him I know the grand nature of this place. Of course, it's beautiful and impressive. But is that all there is? To Tom, it is. That is the measure of success. That is a sign of wellbeing. That is, it. I am not saying that that is all that Tom has to offer, and there must be other levels of dimensions of his worldview. I just have not seen them. Recently Tom was hospitalized with a blocked artery. It was touch and go for a while, but he fully recovered. I asked Tom about that experience. He said, "I've never felt better. I am skiing all the time and feeling great." There was not a window or opening to ask Tom how that experience of near death changed his worldview or belief in a higher power. I am not sure that it did. Or perhaps it has changed, but he's not comfortable talking about that with me. How many Toms do you know? Are you Tom? This book can help you make the shift toward a spiritual worldview that supports your wellbeing.

Going Deeper: We want to feel the emotion that a certain materialistic experience will bring. It is not the fast car, the mansion, or the clothes we can buy. It is the feeling that we get when we have these material things that we are chasing. We can experience spiritual wholeness and an elated sense of wellbeing and connection without the physical or material experience... by retraining and reprogramming the narrative in our minds. I have abundance. I am surrounded by the sacred. I am chosen. I am in wonder and awe.

Transitioning Worldviews

As we move through life, we have different experiences that create or redefine new worldviews. How has your worldview changed over your life course? A Pew Research report indicates that 31% of Americans between the ages of 15 to 29 transitioned from their Christian worldview or belief system to nonaffiliated religious worldviews. I have seen this happen in our own family where youth raised in the church, by Christian values, begin to explore other ways of thinking and believing about the world. Much of this belief comes from social media and TikTok videos. A few years ago, a 19-year-old family member announced she was an atheist. She no longer believed in God or any of the Christian values that she was raised with. Since then, I've witnessed the downward spiral of her mental health, addiction, hopelessness, and despair. I sometimes wonder if this would be different if she had kept believing she is a spiritual being, she is sacred...believing in something. In a world where much is at stake, where we are on the verge of collapse or tremendous growth as a civilization, now is the time to consider how we view the world. Rather than approach worldview as an implicit characteristic that we are born into or live out, we must be intentional about the worldview that we want for our lives, that will help us as spiritual beings with a purpose to love, connect, and walk in wellness and beauty all of the days of our lives. We tend to hang out with people who share a similar worldview. Birds of a feather flock together. Maybe you are not sure about your worldview.

> What do you spend your time thinking and talking about?

> Now that you have read this, how will you apply it in your life?

> What are your Big 8 Social Identities?

> What worldview do you align with the most?

> Name the spiritual teachers and gurus who have influenced your life?

> Where are you on the spiritual continuum and where do you want to be?

Going Deeper: I like to believe that the reason why we have purpose, and we walk toward meaningful acts is that we are being guided by a spiritual force, even if that force is unrealized and unrecognized. If you are not where you want to be spiritually, this is the place to start—knowing that you want to live guided by a different compass and destination than the path you are on.

Identity, Worldviews, Mattering, and Self Love

You might be wondering what worldview has to do with spiritual awakening, and my response is everything. There is a field called the psychology of mattering, the human need to be significant.[22] This field of psychology makes sense to me. I did not find this body of literature until about a year ago when I was designing a research study for individuals with substance use disorders and thought about the concept of mattering. Mattering is associated with connection, affiliation, relationship, social support, and self-esteem. People must remember they matter, they are sacred, they are spiritual, they are on their own path. All of these attributes are part of spiritual wellbeing, and therefore, they matter. Mattering is essential to our health and spiritual wellbeing. It is the root of resilience and connection.

If people do not believe in a spiritual realm, what is their basis for living a physical life? What are they living for? Our belief in the spiritual realm or existence determines how we live our lives here on Earth. If there is no spirit realm, if this is all there is, then why be kind or love others? Here is a story about someone who does not believe in a spiritual existence or realm beyond Earth.

Mark was one of my mentors during my early years as a doctoral student; I was trying to find a path of kindness and purpose, and also trying to satisfy my relentless ego. Mark believed in social justice, equity, fairness, and humanity. But he did not believe in God or an existence beyond the physical or form-based world we experience. He was riding a bike on campus and was hit by a car and driver (texting). He survived the crash but suffered a traumatic brain injury and many broken bones. During this healing journey, post rehab, I would go to the store for him, visit him, and find ways to support him. I did this because I cared for him, and he cared for me. I've moved on and he has retired from the wild, wild world of academia. But I will remember him. He had a birthday recently; he must be nearing 75 or even 80. I wanted to ask him if he had any major epiphany if he had entered the second half of life consciously knowing, but I did not. Some of these things are just too personal and intrusive to ask. As he nears the end of his life, where does he plan to go? What will happen to him? His physical body? His soul? Will I see him again? These are questions I will probably never know the answers to. And that is okay because not everything can be answered regarding matters of the spirit using spoken language. The spiritual dimensions of wellbeing matter because if we do not know what they are, we will not know how to recognize and practice them. They will remain outside of us, outside of the realm of possibility for our lives here on Earth. The spiritual indicators of wellness or the lack of these indicators in various settings, tell us that something must shift in our minds and in our environments if we are to fully embrace mattering and self-love. In this book, we have explored what spirituality looks like and the fact that you are reading this book today tells me that you feel like you matter, you love yourself and spirit.

Mattering is an entire discipline in the field of positive psychology based on the human need to be and feel significant. Because mattering might be an abstract concept for some, researchers have developed the General Mattering Scale (GMS) to assess depression, loneliness, and anxiety to explore what is taking you away from mattering.[22] Answer the questions based on a response of '0' "not at all" to '4' "a lot".

General Mattering Scale

How important are you to others?

How much do others pay attention to you?

How much would you miss if you went away?

How invested are others in what you have to say?

How much do others depend upon you?

Total your score. Remember you are using a 4-point scale where 1 represents "not at all you" and 4 represents "you a lot." Previous studies report that the average GMS score is 16 with a range of 13 and 18. Lower mattering scores related to depression, loneliness, and feelings of insignificance.[23] Studies have found that when adolescents felt like they did not matter to their families, they were more likely to be antisocial, aggressive, and self-destructive. This finding was repeated with 2,000 adolescents. Scores and scales like this are important in beginning to think about where you are at mentally, emotionally, and sometimes spiritually. But these numbers fail to explain how to make the leap from being and feeling insignificant to significant.

Self-love may be the gateway to mattering, spiritual wellness, and consciousness. If we love ourselves, we feel that we matter. We are paying attention to what we need to walk in wellness. We value our own lives even if nobody else does. We are not worried about what others think about us. We find value in the internal vs the external. Self-love is one of the most failed self-care strategies but the most important.

Jane reads emails at all hours of the night. She never stops working. Her physical health is failing her. She rarely takes a shower or wears clean clothes. She is too busy with her job, kids, elderly father, special needs daughter, and a staff of 100 people. Jane is not practicing self-love. She may think that she matters, and she could even score very high on the GMS scale above, but she is unwell physically, spiritually, and emotionally.

What does self-love look like? I have been told over the years that I practice self-care and self-love. This has surprised me because I don't feel that I do, or at least not to the extent that I want to. A good friend of mine is unwell. She matters and scores high on the GMS, but she does not practice self-love. She is constantly criticizing ...body, income, hair, wrinkles, work habits, and how she shows up in the world. She hates who she is. She does not practice self-love. She's been through counseling, therapy, spiritual retreats, and intensive wellness sessions. They have not worked. Why? What can she do?

By now, it might be painfully obvious. Identity and worldview, and the conditioned mind are inextricably linked to our human experience and our spiritual wellbeing. These two areas become foundational in our search for joy, peace, happiness, mattering, and meaning. One of the most challenging things our minds have to do is accept that our worldview is dynamic, complex, changing, and evolving. This makes the conception of spiritual dimensions of wellness difficult to harness in a written book.

There is time. There is hope that together, we can fully tap into our potential as spiritual beings and realize the miracle of life and physical death here on Earth.

To realize that you are not your thoughts is when you begin to awaken spiritually. - Eckhart Tolle

Resources

Big 8 Social Identities

https://www.ochumanrelations.org/wp-content/uploads/2021/01/Big-8-Identities.pdf

Implicit Bias Tests Harvard

https://implicit.harvard.edu/implicit/takeatest.html

Worldviews

https://www.ncbi.nlm.nih.gov/pmc/articles/PMC6735033/#:~:text=A%20worldview%20is%20a%20collection,on%

Reflections for Going Deeper

Read. What did you read about worldviews that you did not know?

Reflect. In what ways might you use these words to become more spiritually awakened?

Remember. What can you remember that matters to you?

Abide. What do you accept?

2 Spiritual Dimensions of Wellbeing

Are you Spiritually Well?

Many people may not consider themselves spiritually well. Some might not believe they have a spirit. But wellbeing is not something that we are, or we aren't. Wellbeing is about our overall existence encompassing the mind, body, spirit, and emotion. Wellbeing is an action, a verb, it is constantly a choice and a flow. This chapter addresses the gap in knowledge of what it means to be spiritually well and the spiritual dimensions of wellbeing. Think back to a time when you were at your best. You felt the healthiest, most balanced, and strong. You might have also felt confident, balanced, grounded, loved, without pain, assured, and joyful.

What was going on in your life at that time?

Who was around you?

What did your daily routine look like?

What helped you be well?

Was there a spiritual dimension to your wellness, or was it merely physical?

We meditate that we might learn to see through Christ's eyes the divine mystery of all that surrounds us. – James Finley

When wellness focuses solely on the physical or form, we become frustrated if and when our bodies fail us. Wellness is a $4 trillion dollar industry in the US. People want to be well, but they don't know how.

So, they buy books, invest in surgeries, hire trainers, go on diets, fast, pray, meditate, do yoga, run triathlons, join therapeutic groups, and more. Health, beauty, and weight loss companies are rebranding to use the terms wellness in their products and advertisements, with the hope that people will buy more, use more, and not actually get well. The issue with the wellness industry is that it largely focuses on the form or external aspects of wellness that will never be quenched by the egoic mind. The egoic mind or egoic self always wants more, it is unquenchable. But we are not our minds. We will talk about happiness later, but just 10 percent of happiness comes from external things (form). This means that 90 percent of our happiness is based on our internal self, what is happening beyond the shell, the thoughts we have, the feelings we feel, the prayers we offer, the connection that we seek and find with the Divine or God. I've always said that happiness is an inside job. Now I know this is true. When we think about wellness, we must think about balance. When we are in balance, all parts work together, and our spirit is at the center, the core of who we are. We can see from this model that when the spirit is unwell, it impacts all aspects of wellness, including our relationships, thinking, behaviors, and feelings/emotions. We can anchor ourselves through balance and these five aspects of self. There will always be challenges to living in a world that is dynamic and unfolding. But there is also a positive interconnectedness between thinking, feeling, behaviors, relationships, and spiritual self that can lessen all brokenness and improve healing, recovery, hope, and joy.

Thinking – cognitive, intellect, thoughts/dialogue in the head

Affect – feelings, emotions, moods, temperament, passions

Behavior – physical, gender, actions, doings

Relational - social connections, family, friends, animals, humanistic, space, generational

Spiritual - Great Mystery, God, Creator, religious or spiritual-based beliefs

Spiritual wellness is not based on your intelligence or strong ties to a specific religious practice. It is based on your life experiences, how you make sense of these experiences, and a deep sense of knowing and being. We do not attain spiritual wellness by reading a book or practicing organized religion. These will fail every time because it's the form not the contents, as Fr. Richard Rohr reminds us. People may rely on religion as a form to feel morally and spiritually superior, but this is a faulty path because no religion that is based in God and of God should do this. When religions make people feel superior to others, this is the ego. Unfortunately, I have encountered many people like this. Before I started on this journey, I thought they were right, and that they were spiritually superior to me. Now I know that they are not and can never be.

Recognizing the Divine

It is not cognition or thinking but recognition or seeing God that changes us. This is why many people have hundreds of books on wellness but for the most part, are unwell. At the same time, it's why people work hard and focus on degrees, houses, cars, and material things because they think that is where happiness and peace will come from. Cognition is why so many brilliant doctors, scientists, engineers, and intellectually gifted people have a difficult time tapping into spiritual ways of living, being, and seeing in the world. You may be no different than these scientists, doctors, and people who seek to make sense of suffering and rationalize what happens when physical death comes. But there are glimpses of recognition of a universal God on this path that many are on. There are moments when we can tap into a universal consciousness and see everything as a gift. In these spaces and experiences, we can tell others to walk in beauty and see everything as a gift, even suffering, frustration, disappointment, and failure. I was visiting with an Elder and friend from the Navajo Nation about this notion of walking in beauty. This is what he said. Walk in beauty, or the people here often use the Red Road of Life. The White Bison Teaching... walk in beauty. When you want that beauty, you are in balance with everything– Mother Earth, air, and the universe. It is the vegetation too. The flowering plants, corn pollen, and flowers produce different pollen. Our feet soak in a mixture of pollen, it will lead us in the beauty way. Same with the moisture, the female and male thunder, we will walk in beauty. When you smell the rain, that is what walking in beauty is about. You enjoy all the things offered to you and given to you. This teaches you about respect. It will make you feel good. Your heart is breathing in the fresh air. Your heart is energized.

This poem by Barbara Holmes speaks to the process of awakening to our fully spiritual and grounded selves:

> I'm cracked open now / No longer drifting Running past their hate and mine / Tipping past "Come here, gal!"... I'm cracked open now / looking for myself, Maybe I spilled into the cleft of the rock / Hiding from the slave catching dogs Maybe I died trying too hard / To birth myself sane I'm cracked, not broken / Still searching for me Amid the shards of God's broken heart. —Barbara A. Holmes, Joy Unspeakable

Spiritual Dimensions of Wellbeing

Spiritual dimensions of wellbeing cannot be packaged in a gift box with a big red bow. They are not static and certainly not tangible or form. But in our English language, we have created words that are indicators of spiritual wellbeing. Here are some examples of what I mean.

Joy and Happiness. Joy is impossible to forget but can be hard to find. Joy is a feeling of extreme happiness. Happiness is a state of being and may include pleasure, contentment, satisfaction, gaiety, glee, good spirits, wellbeing, and enjoyment. A baby is born. A family buys their first car. A relationship is restored. A young woman is the first in her family to graduate from college.

What brings you happiness and joy?

Where in your spirit do you feel joy and happiness?

Gratitude. Everything is a gift, and we deserve nothing. This is a difficult statement to accept, at least at some times in our lives when things are chaotic, stressful, and not going as planned. But we must be grateful. Today the pipes broke in my pump house for the third time. I have no water. There is major water damage everywhere. How am I to practice gratitude during these moments? It was actually simple. I am grateful I noticed the rushing sound of Niagara Falls in my pump house and realized something was wrong. I am grateful I knew how to turn off the breaker to the pump and have a plumber on speed dial with my cell phone charged. I am grateful he answered. I am grateful he is coming to help in just a few hours. I am grateful I have an outhouse to use when the waterline breaks, and the pump fails. This is a practice of simple gratitude that anyone can practice when things do not go as planned.

What does gratitude look like in your life?

How can you practice gratitude and embrace the teaching that everything is a gift?

The answers to this will help you on your path to being spiritually well.

Connection. Everything counts when we are connected to ourselves, the universe, the community, and others. We often seek connection with those with similar energy or interest in spiritual things. I was talking with a colleague about high rates of suicide among youth, a public health crisis that we must address. I asked him why suicide is increasing, especially among our young people. He said it's a lack of connection. Our children have grown up in a digital age with online social media platforms that have not taught them how to socialize, connect, or have meaningful relationships outside the web. When bad things happen, and they will, these youth have no coping mechanisms. They are completely at a loss for who to call, where to go, what to see. Their connections have been disrupted or, in some cases, do not exist. Not all social media is bad, there are some benefits of social connections and help-seeking online, but it is not enough. Just look at the numbers. It is why the US Surgeon General announced that loneliness is an epidemic and a public health crisis killing our population.

Who are you deeply connected to?

How does knowing them awaken your spirit?

Meaning and Purpose. Without meaning and purpose, we falter, fail, depress, and check out. What gives humans meaning and purpose varies based on their social identity, worldview, values, and beliefs. When balancing meaning, purpose, and drive with our egoic mind, we must be careful. Is the thing that gives us meaning and purpose related to praise, recognition, or feelings of superiority? Or is the meaning and purpose tied to service, healing others, and supporting work? There is a fine balance in all of this. Some in the healing profession have the biggest egos of all; they are doing the work because their ego needs to be fed. They have a savior complex and show up as the person with the answers, the expert who holds the keys to recovery. This is simply not the case, but we have bought into this as a society seeking balance and fulfillment in all of the wrong places. I recently worked on a project with a wellness center. The center hired a clinical psychologist to meet with staff weekly and called them advocacy sessions. People showed up and told the psychologist what they wanted to work on. Every week they would meet to review progress. The goal was to understand what gave people meaning, purpose, and connection. We asked participants to complete a survey after the end of every session and at the end of the program when sessions ended. We found that nearly 100% of session participants felt motivated and hopeful because of the sessions. Some responded that sessions gave them meaning, purpose, affirmation, and connection. We did not evaluate the egoic mind of the psychologist.

What gives you spiritual meaning and purpose?

How do you manage your egoic mind?

Deep Knowing. I know what I know, and I have a hard time writing what deep knowing looks like. For example, you might say, "I know God is in me, and I am in God. I know that I am cared for and directed. I know my dreams are a gateway to recognizing my soul as something beyond the physical form. I know that when I die a physical death, I will continue living, and I have always lived. I know that I am chosen and special." But how do you know?

What do you deeply know?

How does this knowledge support your spiritual growth?

Peace. Peace is easy to find when we have it and difficult to get when we do not. Fr. Richard Rohr writes about peace. If we are not centered, focused, or connected, it is easy to be swayed by the conflicts in life—the challenges of the world, war, and injustice. Buddhists remind us that if we want peace, we must be peaceful. Teacher Thich Nhat Hanh instructs us that the path to peace is simple. The only way we are going to be able to create peace in the world is if we first create peace in our hearts. Being peaceful emerges as the path forward through mindfulness practices, meditation, compassion, and contemplation. Peace is a delicate balance of being and doing. Being peaceful is part of the contemplative tradition and teaching. Acting in peace is the process of responding to events when they occur with a non-egoic response with wisdom and empathy toward others.

How do you find peace?

What does being in peace look like in your life?

Compassion. Compassion is suffering with others and offering assistance. Most people run from suffering; they do not want to feel the pain. The way through the pain is in the pain. It might be listening to a coworker who has just experienced disappointment and encouraging them. Or the person at the grocery check-out line who allows you to go ahead of them because you don't have a cart, your hands are full, and the kids are screaming. Self-compassion is part of this. I recently left my daughter standing on a street with a man she barely knew for an hour. I was parked behind a building; she could not see my old car. I could not see her. My phone was dead, and we had no way to communicate. After an hour of waiting, I walked up to where she was supposed to be and saw her looking up at the busy street for my car. She had been staring that way for 60 long minutes. The man was sitting next to her on a bench. She is 14, and the world can be a scary place. When we finally met up, I apologized. I asked her why she didn't walk to the back. That was the location we decided upon. She denied hearing those instructions. This may not seem like that big of a deal in the scheme of things, of life, war, death, and violence. But in our little world, it was big. And as my ruminating and egoic mind often does, I have replayed that event over and over in my mind since it happened. The message woke me early this morning and told me I was not a good mother. This is where self-compassion must come in. I tell myself to breathe. Based on my training and my spirit-led practices I did the following:

> Acknowledge the painful emotion. I am feeling...failure, not enough, not reliable, distracted, unloving. Leaving her on the sidewalk with a man she does not know for an hour makes me feel inadequate as a mother.

> Offer self-compassion statements. May I be loving to myself. May I give myself all of the compassion that I need. May I be strong and learn from this experience.

> Reframe the experience. This was an unfortunate event, but she was safe and not harmed. I am grateful for that.

Try this practice of self-compassion when you feel shame, guilt, or disappointment.

> Acknowledge the painful emotion, what do you feel?

> Offer self-compassion statements, what loving message can you tell yourself?

> Reframe the experience, what is another way to look at what happened?

Service. If there is one religion that understands what it means to serve God, serve humanity, and serve others, it is the Methodists. This book is not intended to convert or promote any religion, but the core beliefs and rules of the Methodist church are: Do no harm. Do good. Stay in love with God. This seems so incredibly simple but, at the same time, difficult as a human being. We attended a Methodist church in New Mexico for about five years, and we learned to serve. Doing good meant serving the community. This church prepped, planned, and served about 200 individuals who experience homelessness every week. Meals were somewhat extravagant and cooked by a team of Methodist followers. The logistics of preparing and serving a meal for 200 in a crowded space with no air conditioning in New Mexico was all about service and doing good. There were times when gunshots were firing outside, cops were coming in to arrest the people, fights were breaking out, drug deals were happening, others were going bad...but also lots of love all around. In our dualistic minds, it is natural to assign a negative or positive emotion to this experience, but that is not possible because it was a blend, there were highs and lows, and the group learned a lot about serving God and serving food to the hungry and homeless. Service of this kind quiets your mind and ego. It is difficult to think about form, the physical realm when people are standing in line for a basic necessity like food. When we have the opportunity to step into these spaces of service to others, we are in a spiritual dimension.

In what ways do you serve others?

How has service connected you to the spiritual path?

Were there times when you felt you were doing something greater than just the physical act of serving others? Did you feel a spirit-to-spirit connection with others?

Going Deeper: All but one of these are non-material or physical dimensions of wellbeing that are felt but not always seen or observed.

This makes it difficult to write about using language, but experiences are the teachers here. The experiences presented demonstrate the process of becoming to know what spiritual wellbeing looks like and is.

Noticing Physical Dimensions

There are pockets of wellbeing in our world. But there is also deep suffering: opioid deaths, car crashes, diseases of despair point to unwellness, and an epidemic of loneliness. People fail to make meaningful connections that encourage an awakened state of being. As a collective, we are uncomfortable being alone, in quiet spaces. Our children and teens are dying early from preventable causes, and our nation is at war with itself and other countries. Conditions fail to promote wellness and offer opportunities to resolve trauma and heal. Climate change is happening right before our eyes with extreme weather events sweeping the globe, fires, droughts, floods, and displacement of communities and nations.

> What does your physical environment look like?

> Do you wake up each morning listening to the birds chirping and stream running, or do you hear traffic, violence, gunshots, or sirens?

> Do you feel physically and spiritually safe?

Safety. It's an essential condition for spiritual wellness. The Centers for Disease Control reviewed the literature on neighborhood violence and safety. Children exposed to violence are more likely to develop poor long-term mental health outcomes, like depression, anxiety, and PTSD. Adult women exposed to violence are more likely to experience depression, disordered eating, and suicidal ideation. Overall, exposure to violence and not being or feeling safe leads to physical, spiritual, emotional, and physical unwellness. It is difficult for individuals to be well if they live in an environment that does not promote wellness. When basic needs are not met, suffering, hustling, and addiction occur.

Poverty. Much of my research and career has focused on the social determinants of health and how conditions add to or take away from wellness. We know that material poverty leads to suffering. We also know that interventions are in place to address this suffering. A few years ago, I was teaching a class on social justice and public health. We reviewed interventions that have a positive impact on addressing poverty. One approach that stands out in my mind is guaranteed basic income programs (GBI). In these programs, people receive a fixed monthly cash payment that allows individuals and families to make their own spending decisions. The city of Stockton, California implemented a GBI program over a 2-year period, the Stockton Economic Empowerment Demonstration Program. Beginning in 2019, the program gave 131 people $500 per month. A control group (those not part of the program but with similar social/economic characteristics) did not receive any money. Findings from this program show that GBI reduces income volatility and psychological distress.[25] Now GBI programs are being replicated in multiple states throughout the US, being lauded as an intervention that has a profound positive impact on public health. While spiritual health or wellness was not studied, it is possible that GBI programs improve spiritual wellness because they address stressful conditions and a lack of material basic needs.

Going Deeper: Walking on a path toward spiritual wellness urges us to focus on what we can control, center, and ground ourselves in who we are as sacred beings, part of a universal consciousness that transcends despair, violence, and poverty.

Observing Physical Dimensions at a Low-Income Clinic

When you look around the room, plane, or home, you are sitting in right now, how many people are well? Do you see joy, connection, meaning, deep knowing, peace, etc., or do you see physical suffering, discontentment, and dysfunction? This week I volunteered at a low-income health and vision clinic with the K-12 schools. I had not spent that much time with that many kids in a while, perhaps ever. I was thinking about their wellbeing, their wellbeing during this time. I wanted to know: Are they well? But how can I say they are well? What indicators are there? I could not see spiritual wellness, just physical indicators of unwellness.

Obesity

We know that 42% of the US population is considered obese, and obesity is increasing at rates we cannot contain. As we get older, we become more obese, and people with college degrees have lower obesity than those without a college education.[26] Obesity can be an indicator of spiritual unwellness, but the research is mixed. For example, a large cohort of adults involved in the Multi-Ethnic Study of Atherosclerosis found that participants with higher religious attendance, prayer, and daily spiritual practices were more likely to be obese than those who were less religious and spiritual. But other studies report no association between spiritual practices and obesity. [27] What we do know is that religious and spiritual connections often promote healthy behaviors, healthier eating, and less consumption of drugs and alcohol.

Kids and Obesity. One in five kids in the US are obese.[28] And the upward trend continues to climb as income decreases; kids who live in poverty are more likely to experience obesity than kids who do not live in poverty. In my subjective observations of obesity at this clinic, only three out of 47 kids were not obese.

Social Media Addiction

Social media is addictive and has harmful effects on the brain, especially among children and teens. On average, they spend nearly 3 hours a day on social media. Constant social media exposure has been linked to anxiety, binge eating, low self-esteem, anxiety, and depression.[29]

I am still at the clinic with the 47 kids. I see one girl on her phone, makeup from Hollywood and YouTube videos. Not from here, is what I think. We walk outside toward the mobile unit, and she is glued to her phone, will not even look up to see where I am taking her, and at a point, I worry she will trip and fall. I ask...

"How do you feel when you get off the phone?"

"Oh, I was just texting my mom."

"How often are you on the phone?"

"All the time."

"How do you feel?"

"I feel bad, I feel horrible after I get off the phone."

"Yes, put the phone down, get outside, and start noticing life that is around you. There is another way to live, beyond the phone."

She was not well. And this is just one high school-aged girl at a clinic I spoke with. I am not her mom or teacher; I am just a volunteer noticing unwellness.

Disability

Up to one in four adults in the US have some type of disability. And the most frequent disabilities reported are related to mobility (12%) and cognition (12%) (thinking, remembering, and making decisions).

We know that individuals who experience disabilities are more likely to experience physical unwellness, including obesity, smoking, heart disease, and diabetes.[30]

I am still at the clinic. I am observing wellness and unwellness. I see an elderly woman and a physically disabled young adult. We begin talking. This is their story. Ruth was born with cerebral palsy at birth. Physically, she is not well. She has limited use of her arms and legs. With a knee brace and stamped leather bag, her grandmother smiles at me as I talk with her. Ruth's graduating from an academy and looking for a job. She's 21, but there are limited jobs or employers who will hire her. They live 21 miles off the main road on the Warm Springs reservation. It's been a rough winter, and she's raising her granddaughter and grandson; their mom is not around. I asked more questions about where they lived. We talked at length about cats, the return of the gray wolf, and gardening. The grandmother was at least 75. I thought about her because she was not well, and she is caring for her granddaughter, who has physical and mental needs. As the primary caregiver, she will one day transition into the non-physical form. She will die a physical death. Her younger grandchildren will be left behind. Who will take care of Ruth after she leaves this Earth? That is the unseen conversation we are having in the waiting room of the vision clinic. It is this knowing that there must be a greater humanity that steps up to help her family. Even if we believe that we are just spiritual beings having a human experience, her family is very human. They have a physical form with human needs that will go unmet without a major shift in how we think about universal wellbeing and taking care of one another.

Going Deeper: When we begin noticing wellness and unwellness around us, we begin connecting and sharing one another's burdens. We cannot take poverty, disability, or obesity away, but we can make people feel known and cared for.

Poverty

Poverty makes us sick and unwell. This is not new information and not that surprising, at least to most people. About 11 percent of the US population lives in poverty and nearly half of these are in deep poverty, meaning that they earned less than half of the poverty threshold. In numbers, this equates to about 37.9 million people.[31] As household income increases, health improves. Many cite greater access to resources, less psychosocial stress, and greater productivity as the reasons for improved health.

At the clinic, I see a girl with heavy black boots approaching the mobile unit. They instruct her to remove the boots, they do not want dirt inside the unit. She refuses to remove the boots. We stood for a while. The story of material poverty is right in front of me. She has crunchy dirty socks on. The boots are worn so badly that the entire top portion or rubber and heel are flapping and sticking to the ground while she walks. Her clothes have not been washed, maybe ever. This girl does not have access to a washer and dryer. She does not smell good. The dog chain with sharp edges around her neck sends a message, get away from me. I am tough. I can hurt you. We found plastic crocs and clean socks in the school clothes donation bin. The sky-blue crocs are too big, but the socks are clean. She reluctantly gives us her boots and dirty socks, puts on the new shoes, and walks up the stairs to the clinic. She is embarrassed. Feels shame. Knows she is being judged. I watch her walk through the clinic and through her life. I can see the difficulties that she will encounter because she experiences material poverty. There is nothing in her thinking that relates to spirituality. She is not concerned about spiritual wellness. She does not have shoes, access to water, or food.

These stories point to a huge gap in how we approach wellness in our world. We have focused so much on physical unwellness that we do not know what actual wellness looks like in physical form, and we certainly do not know what it looks like in spiritual form. How could we? We have gone down the wrong road. Western medicine fails. The US is becoming more and more irrelevant and unconscious. When will we begin noticing spiritual wellbeing, that there is more to who we are, beyond the physical form? When we answer this question, we will solve the physical, mental, emotional, and spiritual crisis that we are living in. Everything begins and ends with our spirit.

Noticing Spiritual Wellbeing

Think about the most spiritually well person that you know.

> What tells you that they are spiritually well?

> Are they a priest, guru, monk, religious zealot?

> Do they pray all of the time, meditate, shave their heads?

> How do they make you feel?

> What makes you think they have a sacred identity and transcended as a spiritual human being?

While I would love to know your responses to these questions, it is not possible. Let me tell you about some commonly accepted indicators of spiritual wellbeing. Indicators of spiritual wellbeing are everywhere and nowhere. If we are looking at the spiritual indicators of wellbeing, we have to consider what it looks like and feels like. This starts with values and what we value. How do we live out our values in our daily lives? Deepak Chopra's book Living in the Light describes what it means to live in the light as a conscious individual with spiritual wellbeing.32 According to his wisdom, three things happen when people are spiritually awakened or, I would add, spiritually well. First, people lose fear of death. Second, they practice and live platonic values, like truth, goodness, beauty, and harmony. Third, people realize their consciousness does not exist in space-time, they transcend to a universal being and deep knowing that is not divided by space and time. All experiences happen within the spirit, not outside of the spirit as individual occurrences. Here, space-time refers to the space we occupy in the world, the world is in us. Stillness emerges as an indicator that we are occupying more than just the physical realms of thinking and doing. Here are some stories of these indicators based on real-world experiences.

Three Signs of Spiritual Wellbeing

#1- Lost fear of death. A friend was diagnosed with colon cancer. She was in her 60s at the time of diagnosis. She had lived a full life as an artist, grandmother, and social worker. She was active in tribe's ceremonies and routinely fasted, prayed, and attended the sweat lodge. But cancer changed this. She was confined to her home, relied on other people for continuous care, and endured multiple rounds of chemotherapy. After she completed her treatments, I asked her about death. I wanted to know if she was afraid to die, or ready to die. She said, 'I am not afraid of death. I have known many people who have died and came back to Earth. They told me that we are going to a beautiful place. That I have nothing to fear. I welcome death.' This story has been told to me in different ways over the years. When people advance in physical age and spiritual maturity, they are no longer afraid to die.

#2- Platonic values. These values come from experience and a genuine desire to know good, truth, beauty, love, harmony, joy, gratitude, and humility. It is somewhat rare to find someone who embodies all of these qualities at the same time. But there are glimpses of these values in people who are spiritually well. Julie was 18 when she got married.

She never went to college and wanted to be a stay-at-home mom, never working outside the house. She married John and together they had two kids, one experienced a physical and mental disability. Over the years, I would see the family at our church. I was always amazed at how joyful, truthful, and humble Julie was, well all of them. Her platonic values were anchored in her deep Christian faith and religious beliefs. I never asked her, but I cannot help but think that she was having spiritual experiences at church.

#3 Transcendence. Spiritual transcendence may look different depending on who and where you are. It is not constant, at least not for most people. There are spaces in-between physical experiences where people transcend. Most transcendence occurs with relinquishing of the ego, realizing we are not our egos, and we are not our conditioned minds, or the stories we make up and tell ourselves about the world around us and what is happening to us. Because spiritual transcendence is deeply personal and not always communicated in a verbal or written form, it can be difficult to identify. For some people, transcendence happens when they remind themselves that the universe is in them, they are not in the universe. It is a deeply felt connection to God and a knowing that brings feelings of peace, joy, bliss, and serenity. You may be driving down a gravel road listening to Eckhart Tolle telling you that you are not your thoughts or your egoic mind. That everything that is happening right now is the way that it should be, and you are bigger than your car, body, job, bank account, or any number of egoic accomplishments. This is a way of knowing. Transcendence occurs when we become free of the person we identify with as ourselves.

I have experienced transcendence walking on fresh white snow in the forest on a path leading to nowhere. Greeting the sun shining through the clouds and trees, it's a message from God, just for me. Animals in the wild greet me like I am one of them, the red fox running his race crossing the road, the mountain lion staring into my eyes, reminding me I am a guest in his home. Walking into a gym, filled with families, kids, and loud noises... feeling alive, chosen, special, powerful, and grounded (even when the visible world may not notice my existence).

When and where have you experienced transcendence?

Can you predict when it will happen?

Do you physically feel something? (chills, goosebumps, etc.)

A Wolf in Sheep's Clothing

Jessie is our 4-year-old Australian Shepherd. She is beautiful with perfect markings, human eyes, and the softest fur. She looks like a giant teddy bear, but she is not. She despises strangers or people who are not part of our core family. Workers come, church groups come, helpers come, and Jessie wants to kill them or at least attack them to the point where they cannot hurt her and the core family. There are many reasons why Jessie acts this way. I am not a dog therapist or trainer, but I've been told it's in their breed–the anxiety and need to protect the herd/core family at all costs. Jessie is similar to some of the people you may have met in your life who profess to be spiritual, they have titles and positions that make you think that they are among the elite and spiritually well. But they are deeply unwell. We cannot view spiritual wellbeing dualistically, as either you possess it, or you do not. Things are not black and white. There are spaces in between spaces that show us that God can live in people, even when they are acting like a wolf in sheep's clothing. Here are some examples of Jessies I have known.

Catholics Showing Spiritual Emptiness

I am not Catholic, but you might be. No matter what you are or where you are, you are probably aware of the gross and negligent history of the catholic church. Sexual abuse, genocide, lying, stealing, cheating, just about every sin that is in the Bible, they have committed, and committed in a big way. Now we must not throw stones, all of us have lived in a glass house at one time or another. But people sought out the Catholic church because it was a place where they went to find spiritual connections, guidance, meaning, and forgiveness. It is difficult to go even a week without reading a new headline about the Catholic church and new cases of sexual abuse against priests. Just last week the headline read, "600 children sexually abused by the Baltimore Catholic Church over 60 years". What is most repulsive about these instances is that the sexual abuse cases were covered up, denied, and rejected by the church until it was no longer possible to argue with the evidence provided by the attorney general's office and the testimonies of these children, now adults. The priests were spiritually unwell. The church was spiritually unwell. How do we know this? The actions of abuse, the lack of accountability, and the unwillingness of these individuals and this system to admit wrongdoing. Some in the Catholic Church feel that God brought the exposure of sexual abuse cases and violence to light... reminding the church that they are not above the rules of do no harm... do good... love one another as Christ loves us.

Elders Being Unkind, Missing Platonic Values

Many believe that most Elders and grandparents are spiritually well. We can create stories in our minds, if someone lives long enough, they will have knowledge, wisdom, and lessons that will contribute to their spiritual wellbeing. But this is not always the case. Elders are not always spiritually well. For example, I know an Elder that is an executive of a youth serving organization. She practices meditation, contemplation, prayer, attendance, and religious activities. Externally, she appears spiritually well. She is doing everything on the outside that would point to spiritual wellness. But she is not well in that way. She is unkind to people, unclear, and her ego drives every decision that she makes. When I look at her, I do not feel sincerity. There is nothing heartfelt about her, I cannot see the realm of the heart within her. I am not God. I am just noticing the wolf in sheep's clothing.

Jim, another Elder, was on his deathbed, dying of cancer. He was an angry spiritually unwell person, who treated his family and others poorly. He was consumed with material goods, status, and fame. The last few days of his life he spent alone. His wife and sons did not want to be with him. He never found platonic values, and this was evident in how he lived, right up until his final breath.

Psychics Preying on the Unwell

A friend of mine regularly uses a psychic. Their conversations occur over the phone, and the psychic tells her things about the future. What will happen in her life and the life of her family and friends. She pays the psychic $425 per session. Sometimes the psychic will call her and ask to schedule a session, there is something the psychic knows that she wants to share with my friend. People who take your money to tell you about your possible future are not spiritually well. They are preying on the vulnerabilities of humans who are suffering, unwell, and uncertain about the future.

Clinicians Not Awakened

Counselors and doctors are not by default, spiritually well. There is not a screening process when they enter their degree programs or professions asking about their spiritual practices or overall wellness. There are psychological screening tools, background checks, ethics statements, but no spiritual wellness assessments. Mainstream America believes that doctors and counselors hold the keys to their wellness and recovery. In fact, our Western medical system relies on these professions to survive. They may prescribe antidepressants for feelings of unwellness but never ask what is making a person unwell and depressed to begin with. When a prescription leaves a doctor's office without notice of the conditions that are causing depression or unwellness, this is an indicator that the prescribing doctor is unaware, unconscious, and not spiritually attuned to what creates wellness at the individual and universal level. Many in these professions do not know how to live, work, and act in a different way. They are focused on a path of physical wellness, eliminating disease, ending health disparities, alleviating physical pain, and suffering. But there is more to wellness than these physical dimensions.

Professors and Their Egos

When I was completing my doctoral degree, one of my advisors told me that most people enter into the field of psychology, psychotherapy, and counseling because they want to make sense of their own minds, upbringing, and dysfunction. I recall thinking about that and looking at him. He was brilliant by academic standards, he had everything a tenured professor could want - millions of dollars in research, a dozen graduates and PhD students working for him, and hundreds of publications. But he was spiritually and physically unwell. He contracted a rare virus which limited his ability to speak, he was near death at several points throughout his hospital stay. Some students went to visit him in the hospital, they felt bad that he did not have family or friends to care for him. I did not. I signed a card, but that was it. When he returned to the university several months later, he was the same egoic human, the near-death experience did not change him. He continued to treat people poorly and berate people, junior faculty, and students, and those around him. I never learned his complete life story but there was trauma, abandonment, and a lack of attachment to his parents and loved ones. He brought his dysfunction and unwellness to the classroom and projects we worked on. He was not trustworthy or safe. These were indicators of his lack of spiritual wellbeing.

Researchers Without Recovery

Many people in the recovery community are put on pedestals for their sobriety, and rightly so. They have overcome wicked addictions and trauma and lived to talk about it. But not all people in recovery are spiritually well. This is what I mean. I have been sober for more than three years. I am in long-term recovery. But there was a time early in my recovery, maybe 6 months in, that I was angry. I was angry because I could not drink, and angry because I wanted to. I work with recovery organizations and treatment programs. I would regularly show up to meetings and sessions hungover from the night before. My colleagues, many of whom work in these programs, drank with me. I was living two lives. One life was as a researcher and advocate for recovery and sobriety, the other life was consuming bottles of expensive red wine and not thinking twice that I was a hypocrite. I had to get angry with myself to stop drinking. When I decided to stop, I told myself, I will just try it for a week. A week turned into a month, and a month turned into a year. The wild thing about this process was that I never considered myself an "addict" or person in recovery. I was the person who held the keys to recovery and told people who could recover and what they needed to recover. It is painful looking back on the journey, but it is the truth. Anyone who is walking on the Red Road of wellness knows that truth is all there is. Years later, the anger has subsided. I am not angry anymore, just grateful. Platonic values are showing up more and more and I finally see things in life for how they are and where they are, without a worldview or lens that is tainted by alcohol. My Earthly experience is based on deep knowing, a relationship with an existential being, and a belief in a universal God. This would not have been possible when I was actively drinking. I seek and practice non judgment, non-attachment, and non-reactivity. It is difficult but the only way of seeking and being well.

Healers Needing Healing

I recently completed studies with recovery organizations, outpatient facilities serving individuals and families in early and long-term recovery. We asked employees to rate their overall wellness using the medicine wheel concepts of spirit, mental, physical, and emotional. We found that overall, these groups were mentally and spiritually well (they ranked these domains of wellness the highest), but physical wellness was ranked the lowest. This was consistent across groups, in different organizations with similar staff and training. What this tells me is that they have spent so much time working on their spiritual wellness, that they have limited time for physical. This observation is evident in heart disease, obesity, diabetes, and an array of physical ailments. Many people are spiritually well but physically unwell. My work in communities throughout the US over two decades has taught me a lot about the conditions that support spiritual wellness and unwellness. I have observed ceremonies, rites of passage, fasting, prayer, dances, celebrations, and dinners - activities that feed the spirit and connect the mind to a sense of sacred identity and belonging. But the presence of these celebrations and ceremonies in a community does not always mean people are spiritually well. Many of these communities suffer from addiction, unresolved trauma, grief and loss, and generational poverty.

Going Deeper: External appraisals of spiritual gurus may be all right or all wrong. We should not judge people by their titles, degrees, or status. We must consider the seeds people plant. The way they make us feel. The dimensions of true self drop when titles, egoic frames, and the physical form leaves.

Emotions and Feelings

How we think and feel relates to our spiritual wellbeing. At a very basic level, feelings can be categorized as angry, happy, or sad. We might feel peaceful, surprised, or fearful. Or powerful, excited, or shame.

Whatever feeling you are feeling, it is okay to feel it. When our needs are being met and we feel spiritually well, we might experience appreciation, confidence, peace, inspiration, and gratitude. If you are not feeling the way that you want to feel, you can change the emotion or feeling by countering it with an activity that brings you the desired state of being. For example, if you feel depressed or anxious, do things that make you feel capable, confident, and grounded. For some, this may be working in my gardens or reading a book. If you feel lonely or in isolation, seek opportunities to serve others, join a church, volunteer at a local non-profit, or seek and find God. These are all things that we can do on our own to reframe and retrain our feelings and emotions about our lives and current situations.

> What is the most common emotion you experience during the day?

> What do you feel right now?

> What are your thoughts preceding the feeling you have?

Researchers have studied the circuits of the brain that cause undesirable emotions. David Anderson is a Professor of Biology at Caltech who studies the brain and emotional behaviors with animals.[33-34] His research demonstrates a connection between animal and human emotions. Because emotions are a function of the brain that have evolved over time, he argues that human brains are similar to those found in mice and fruit flies. His studies show that if we can look beyond human feelings and into the circuits of the brain, we can address trauma, fear, aggression, and other undesirable experiences. But our brains are flawed and can create intense negative emotions based on our environment and conditions. Where is the spirit in these studies and this process? We cannot easily dissect spirit and memories like we can a mouse brain or that of a microscopic fruit fly. But if we smile or even imitate a smile, this changes the neural circuits in our brain related to emotional content.

Researchers studied the smiles of students in yearbooks over a 30-year period.[35] They wanted to know if smiles were a good indicator of student wellbeing and success throughout their lives. Researchers explored how fulfilling and long lasting their marriages would be, how high they would score on standardized tests that measure wellbeing, general happiness, and how inspiring they would be to others. Their results blew me away. The students with the biggest and widest smiles ranked highest in all of these categories, every time, over a 30-year period. Another study extended this research and looked at smiles and life expectancy. Researchers found that smiles increased life expectancy in one study group from 72.9 years to 79.9 years (a seven-year difference).

Just a smile. Scientists think that smiling stimulates the brain and reward mechanisms similar to chocolate, exercise, and other pleasure-inducing activities in the brain.

When you smile do you look and feel good?

When others see you smile, do they smile back?

Why not smile more?

Brains and Survival

Our minds create narratives about thoughts, stories, predictions, memories, and judgements about things happening all around us. We have five senses: vision, hearing, touch, smell, and taste. These senses are parts of our brain and the strongest are seeing and hearing. Our brain does not know the difference between emotions and feelings, it is simply sorting through the computer hard drive of our brains to tell us, "This is a threat run, or This is okay, stay calm, relax." In some of our research, we explore the fight or flight response that humans have to adverse experiences and trauma. Trauma disconnects our spirits from our physical bodies and brain. The amygdala is part of our brain that identifies threats or danger (physical or emotional trauma). It activates our brain through our sympathetic nervous system. The nervous system then releases stress hormones and chemicals like cortisol and adrenaline. We might feel stress and anxiety during or after a traumatic event. But our brains are limited and sometimes they send faulty alarms, triggered by past traumas or built in survival instincts.

Are You Ready?

Readiness is something we must consider on the path to awakening the spirit. Not everyone is ready to walk toward the spiritual dimensions of wellness. They are working on other dimensions of wellness, or they don't feel they have the time or resources to do so.

Research on readiness for change is long and deep. One model that is used a lot in communities and healing spaces is the transtheoretical model of change. Originally developed by Prochaska and DiClemente,[36] this model walks us through the steps of readiness and urges us to look closely at where we are both physically and spiritually, and where we want to be. It begins with thinking, or precontemplation and ends with maintenance.

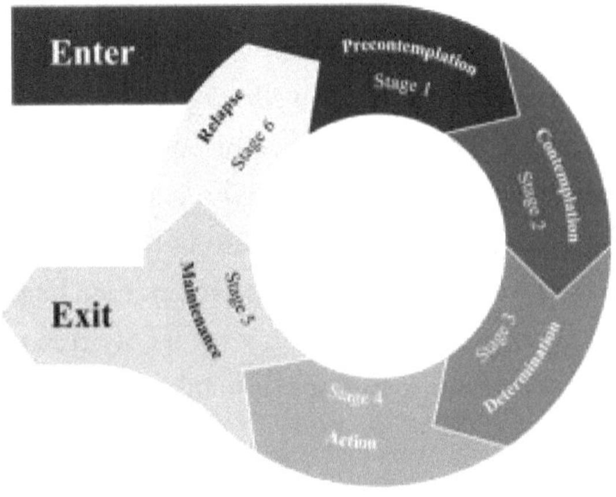

You will be ready to consider these spiritual dimensions when everything else has failed. When you have stepped into the great abyss and did not find what you were looking for...when the new car and big house did not quench your thirst. Sometimes this means you have suffered in some way. You are not happy or content with life as we know it. You hit rock bottom. You are in the dark hole of life and cannot find your way out. This is a sign that change is possible and needed.

74

It's through these experiences that we find out what we need to be spiritually well.

In rare instances, humans will escape suffering, the dark holes of life. They will not hit rock bottom looking for a way out. They will continue with the status quo of their life, which may be fine, mediocre, or amazing. The spiritual dimensions of wellbeing will come to humans when they are ready for something different. When life as we know it no longer fulfills the spirit's desire for wholeness, connection, joy, and blessings. This is the ultimate goal. When we have and practice the spiritual dimension of wellbeing in our lives, we can then begin to share these with others. Sharing is not always in a verbal, written or physical form, it is prayerful, universal, a balance of being and action, and deep knowing.

Resources

National Public Radio, Smiling Tricks Your Brain into Happiness

https://www.nbcnews.com/better/health/smiling-can-trick-your-brain-happiness-boost-your-health-ncna822591

Social Media Disorder Scale https://www.sciencedirect.com/science/article/pii/S0747563216302059#appsec1

Stages of Change

https://sphweb.bumc.bu.edu/otlt/mph-modules/sb/behavioralchangetheories/behavioralchangetheories6.html

World Happiness Study

https://worldhappiness.report/ed/2023/world-happiness-trust-and-social-connections-in-times-of-crisis/

Reflection for Going Deeper

Read. What did you read that speaks to your own stage in life?

Reflect. In what ways might you use these words to reframe how you practice the spiritual dimensions of wellbeing?

Remember. What can you remember that matters to you?

Abide. What do you accept?

3 Evidence For the Spirit

I s it Real?

What evidence do we have that the spiritual realm exists? What evidence do we need to make the case about spiritual wellbeing? This chapter addresses the perspective that there is no evidence for the spiritual realm, and there is no reason for awakening. Seeking evidence for spirituality looks different based on where you stand. Embracing the knowledge that we are spiritual beings having a human experience is the first step in understanding the spiritual realm. The spiritual realm (that which is formless, non-material, and not easily defined by language) is only known by those who experience it. We can know things or believe them, but never experience them. This is why many people seek evidence of the spiritual realm in external people, places, and things. People work an entire year, save money, fly across the ocean to a sandy beach in Hawaii, seeking peace, connection, and the Divine. Oftentimes people are seeking the Spirit without knowing that the spiritual realm is inside of them, it is part of who they are as spiritual beings connected to a Divine creator and maker of the universe, all things. The spiritual and physical world is vast, diverse, and dynamic.

The spiritual realm is the gathering place for the souls of all people... A realm of this size of course, contains countless phenomena that people on Earth have never imagined. – Emanuel Swedenborg, Secrets of Heaven

You, or someone you know and love, may seek and have found evidence for spiritual (or non-form) existence in various pockets of the universe. Consider people who are slightly obsessed with spiritual wellbeing and the spiritual realm based on these things, practices, and teachings.

Religion

Out of Body and Near-Death Experiences

Supernatural or paranormal

Ghosts

Tarot card readers

Psychics

Hallucinogenic

Research

Many others

Religious evidence seekers may look to the Bible for confirmation that they are indeed spiritual beings having a physical or human existence. In Genesis 1:27, the teaching is, "God created man in his own image, in the image of God he created him; male and female, he created them." Christians believe in both the spirit realm and spiritual warfare. Paul in Ephesians 6:12 writes, "The struggle is not against flesh and blood but against evil forces in the heavenly and Earthly realms." Jesus cast out demons from the sick in Mark 1:32, "Jesus healed many people who were sick with various diseases, and he cast out many demons. But because the demons knew who he was, he did not allow them to speak." But exorcisms are not just limited to Christianity. Buddhism, Judaism, Islam, and Hinduism have practiced exorcisms throughout history.

Some experience out of body experiences or near-death experiences (NDEs). While someone who experiences an NDE often does not want to experience it, they often come back from their NDE with insights into consciousness, evidence that an afterlife does exist, and are transformed in some way based on the experience.

One book that literally changed what I think about belief and life after death, or the final journey home is Eben Alexander's book, Proof of Heaven.[37] As a self-proclaimed atheist and trained neuroscientist, he believed that faith was just brain chemistry and that our souls were a product of this chemistry, and nothing more. But when Alexander contracted a rare medical condition, he was in a coma for seven days. During this time, Alexander describes a slow spinning white light of great clarity associated with music, a subterranean realm leading to a valley filled with colors and light that are not seen on Earth. Moving through the valley, he describes his experience as a speck of awareness on a butterfly wing where thoughts of unconditional love and assurance were part of awareness. Alexander met an angelic being who took him to heaven. He met the Divine source of the universe itself, the Creator. Just as the doctors were considering stopping his treatment, he woke up. Now he believes in the Divine Creator of the universe. He has come to know, tell, and publish, that the brain does not create consciousness. He believes that we are conscious even without our brains. Alexander firmly believes that health, and I would add wholeness and enduring well, are only achieved when we embrace the Creator, the Divine, God.

There are other stories too, told to me by friends. A good friend died, went to heaven, and came back. The doctors pronounced him brain dead. During this time, he transitioned into heaven. He told me about the colors in heaven, the bright light and love, he did not want to return to Earth. Another friend had a similar experience.

There are many spiritual, religious, and faith-based explanations and theories about why we should believe in the Divine. Eben Alexander's is just one. Explanations and stories are deeply personal, and closely mirror writing or discussing politics. I make it a point to never discuss politics because I realize that one's individual views about politics are their own, they are not mine, and they are not mine to change. People will vote, change, and believe based on their own journey, not a book, banner, or march. It is about choice. We must have conversations about beliefs on the healing path, God, suffering, and death.

Supernatural teachings and experiences lead to evidence for spirituality. In Japan, the Shinto beliefs indicate that a soul or spirit lives within all existence and phenomena. Household objects like plants, animals, or cups are viewed as deities. They believe that the connection between the physical and spiritual world teaches people about respect. Consider the example of a cup that is a vessel of an ancestor. You would not throw the cup out if you knew it held the spirit of your great grandfather.

Ghosts (or the formless) are evidence for some that the spiritual realm is near and here. An estimated 57% believe in ghosts and 49% have felt the presence of a ghost in their lifetime. [38] Stories of ghost sightings and encounters are frequent in the mainstream media and in our history. Netflix shows on the paranormal give insight into how people experience the formless, although some of these shows lack a strong evidence base. Ghost tours of haunted houses are common in most major cities in the US. My niece decided one year that she would apply to be a ghost tour guide in a central Oregon town. She memorized her script, dressed up as a gothic character, and walked people through a ghost tour of buildings thought to be occupied by ghosts. I asked her about this experience after the gig was over. "Yes, it's real. These places are occupied by ghosts...it's freaky," she said. She learned to memorize a script while meeting ghost seekers from around the globe and made good tips. Other stories of ghosts encountered throughout history are common. Winston Churchill returned from World War II and was staying at the White House. He just finished having a bath and walked into the adjoining bedroom where he was met by the ghost of Abraham Lincoln. Churchill greeted Mr. Lincoln who smiled and then vanished.

Tarot card readers can be found in any major city, at local fairs, online, and throughout the world. Some profess that tarot card reading is the connection to the spiritual realm. In this practice, cards are placed in a spread, then interpreted based on the value and position in the spread. Readings may address specific problems or future events that occur.

Psychic mediums can help people connect to a spiritual realm. The goal of most mediums is to help people gain spiritual wellbeing and inner peace. Many spiritual seekers consult psychic mediums to get in touch with their loved ones. The show on Netflix, Life After Death with Tyler Henry illustrates his psychic abilities. Watching this, one observes how his skills have been used to find missing and murdered persons, solve crimes, and give families solace in their grief. If you are not a believer in psychic abilities, this show might change your way of thinking about mediums. A friend went to a psychic. They told her to sell everything she owned and move to Hawaii. Another colleague went to a psychic for career advice. They told her to quit her job and buy an R.V. to live in. She did that. In both cases, life became hard for them. There was freedom in packing up all of their worldly goods, but there was deep loss and in some cases hardship, poverty, and distress.

Psychedelics have been used for thousands of years to unlock the unconscious mind and heal the physical body from addiction, disease, and disconnection to spirit. They are increasingly being used to treat depression and individuals with severe mental illness. For example, ketamine and psilocybin are used to treat depression, anxiety, post-traumatic stress disorder, and substance use disorders. Evidence suggests that psychedelics work because they release oxytocin in the brain which often creates feelings of trust, and closeness that helps individuals connect with their spirit and with others who want to help them (counselors, therapists, family).

[Mystical experiences are] those peculiar states of consciousness in which the individual discovers himself to be one continuous process with God, with the Universe, with the Ground of Being, or whatever name he may use by cultural conditioning or personal preference for the ultimate and eternal reality. – Alan Watts

Mapping the Evidence

Researchers use the scientific method, randomized controlled studies, and various clinical experiments to build an evidence base for the spiritual realm and spiritual wellbeing. There are millions of ways to create a map of the evidence for spiritual existence and spirituality. After considering how people seek the spiritual realm and the evidence that exists for these practices, we may not agree with them. We may be fearful or adamant that they do not work or do not exist. But people are all seeking similar things, just in different ways. For example, many researchers find extreme comfort in quantifying phenomena to make sense of what is happening, or to prove or disprove a certain theory or hypothesis. Many have big questions and seek answers. At the beginning of this book, we reviewed worldviews and researcher positionality. Worldviews drive our perceiving, thinking, knowing, and doing. They are about senses, faith, and actions in the world. Every researcher, someone who is creating evidence about spiritual wellness, has a worldview. Their worldview influences research evidence, outcomes, and how evidence is disseminated, even if they try to be objective and follow strict research protocols.

Going Deeper: Evidence for the spiritual realm and spiritual practices is everywhere. There are many roads that lead to spiritual knowing and transcendence. When assessing the evidence and following people with self-proclaimed evidence, be cautious. There are many people walking this Earth who are not awakened, but merely want to prey on those who are lost, seeking the Divine, and wanting connection.

Many years ago, I walked into a friend's office who was an epidemiologist. She had a sign positioned above her desk, "If you cannot measure it, it does not exist." This was her thinking for a long time. As a researcher, I am slightly obsessed with measuring things. Quantifying or qualifying large bodies of work to make a statement about something, prove causality, show an effect, or publish a paper. I know this is essentially my egoic identity showing up because none of this seems remotely spiritual, transcendent, or existential. Let's agree, for now, that quantifying spirituality and or spiritual wellbeing matters in the scheme of human existence. Multiple spiritual wellbeing scales have been developed and validated. Examples include the spiritual wellbeing scale, the multidimensional measurement for religiousness and spirituality, and the spiritual life and health orientation measure. All of these have the same goal: to measure spiritual wellbeing, and possibly do something about it. Consider the following questions on the spiritual wellbeing scale developed by Paloutzian and Ellison in 1982.[39] An "E" after each statement measures existential wellbeing being, an "R" after each statement measures religious wellbeing. Respond to each statement using a 5- point scale where 1 represents strongly disagree and 5 strongly agree. Answer the questions based on a response of '1' "strongly disagree" to '5' "strongly agree". Combined, these create a spiritual wellbeing score that often ranges from 10 to 50. A higher score represents a higher level of spiritual wellbeing, and a lower score represents a lower level of spiritual wellbeing.

Spiritual Wellbeing Scale

E= Existential, R= Religious

I know who I am, where I come from, and where I am going. -E

I believe that God loves me and cares about me. - R

I have a personally meaningful relationship with God. -R

I feel very fulfilled and satisfied with my life. -E

I get personal strength and support from God. -R

I believe that God is concerned about my problems. -R

I feel good about the future. -E

My life has meaning. -E

My relationship with God contributes to my sense of wellbeing. -R

I believe there is some real purpose in my life. -E

The problem with scales like this one is that spiritual wellbeing is dynamic, not static. Scores change based on life experiences and conditions. If someone is having a really bad day, they may have a difficult time scoring a 5 on the statement, "I believe that God is concerned about my problems." In the darkest times, they may feel that God does not even exist. But a few weeks might go by, they are feeling positive, fulfilled, loved by the Creator of the universe. The score then jumps from a 0 to a 5, the highest level of agreement for spiritual wellbeing. Empirical evidence comes from experience and observation. It may also come from clinical, biological, behavioral, epidemiological, social, or even spiritual studies and realms. Scientific research often leads to empirical evidence. We know and observe the sun setting every day of our lives, even on cloudy days when we cannot see the sunset. We know this is true because we experience this happening every day. We can observe the outside temperature on a thermometer, it tells us how hot or cold it is on a given day. No matter who is looking at the temperature, it will remain the same. This is an example of empirical evidence from observation. Empirical evidence is also available that demonstrates a direct connection between religious involvement, spirituality, and positive health outcomes. This body of research or evidence demonstrates that spiritual practices increase life expectancy, lower blood pressure, lessen depression, lessen severe medical problems, and lead to a better quality of life.[40] This section is dedicated to evidence, for the critics, or those who may believe that the spiritual realm and spiritual wellbeing are woo-woo topics, not grounded in any evidence. Here are some examples of published evidence from researchers.

Human Minds Convert Possibility to Reality

Consider the famous two-slit experiment. When you watch a particle go through the holes, it behaves like a bullet, passing through one slit or the other. If no one observes the particle, it exhibits the behavior of a wave and can pass through both slits at the same time. This and other experiments tell us that unobserved particles exist only as "waves of probability" as the great Nobel laureate Max Born demonstrated in 1926. They're statistical predictions — nothing but a likely outcome. Until observed, they have no real existence; only when the mind sets the scaffolding in place can they be thought of as having duration or a position in space. Experiments make it increasingly clear that even mere knowledge in the experimenter's mind is sufficient to convert possibility to reality.

As Kant pointed out over 200 years ago, everything we experience — including all the colors, sensations, and objects we perceive — are nothing but representations in our mind. Space and time are simply the mind's tools for putting it all together. Now, to the amusement of idealists, scientists are beginning to dimly recognize that those rules make existence itself possible. Indeed, the experiments above suggest that objects only exist with real properties if they are observed. The results not only defy our classical intuition but suggest that a part of the mind — the soul — is immortal and exists outside of space and time.

Have the courage to use your own understanding. – Immanuel Kant

Quantum physics is a field of study that I know absolutely nothing about. The idea that I am sitting at a coffee shop right now reading about the famous double-slit experiment and Schrodinger's Cat might make you question my credibility and authority to write this book. But there are some things we can learn about the spiritual and non-form world from these experiments, without being quantum physicists. Researchers in Poland explored the relationship between spirituality, health-related behaviors, and psychological wellbeing with 595 college students. They found that spirituality and health-related behaviors are positively related to psychological wellbeing. This confirms previous empirical studies that found spiritual wellbeing is positively correlated with emotional and existential wellbeing and protective against depression.[41] Religion and spirituality are often combined in research studies because they are related to similar yet distinct constructs. A systematic review of more than 188 publication articles [42] on religion and health found empirical research which focuses on health behaviors, substance abuse, coping and adjustments related to growth, dementia prevention or coping, psychological wellbeing, prayer, mortality and longevity, physical health, discrimination, environmental health, infection disease, crime and delinquency, family, youth, and reproductive outcomes, training among health professionals and religious leaders, spiritual wellbeing at the end of life, referral and adherence, programs for prevention and treatment, organizational factors, treatment and interventions, mental health and disorders, patient psychosocial wellbeing, sources of spiritual wellbeing, doctor-patient conversations, perspectives at the end of life, and specific religious traditions. While it is impossible to review all of these studies, the point is that the spiritual realm (or non-quantifiable weird realm), spirituality, and religion have a scientific evidence base, and this evidence base tells us that the spiritual dimensions of health matter.

A colleague of mine was interviewed recently about her spiritual practices and how they impact her work. She is younger than me, creative, and seems to be an okay human. I don't know her well. Listening to the interview, she said, "I don't believe in God. I guess you could say I am agnostic. I don't think there is anything but the physical realm, here on Earth. The goal is just to get up each day and try your best. Do your best, and if you don't do well, you have another day to try." That was the end of the interview, and I was shocked. I imagined being her, not having a belief in anything spiritual, that God did not exist, and our lives here on Earth were merely physical. Has she not read the dual slit experiment or watched the dead cat with Schrodinger? I should not be thinking about these things, but I am. Part of this belief has to do with one's psychological maturity and life course, are they in the first half or second half of life? These concepts will be introduced later in this text. After considering all of this, you might be wondering what evidence for the spiritual realm has to do with spiritual wellbeing? My answer is everything. But there are many paths to access the spiritual realm, and these paths are as wide as the ocean is deep.

Evidence For Contemplation and Meditation to Access the Spiritual Realm

Meditation and contemplation are being used in the wellness industry, among treatment centers, and in most therapeutic offices throughout the world. One common requirement of contemplation and meditation is that they require an attentiveness to the spirit of God (and many other names for God). Contemplation helps us build deep awareness, being present with the heart, mind, and body. Some pray or meditate to connect with God. Fr. Richard Rohr describes contemplation in the best way.

Contemplation is entering a deeper silence and letting go of our habitual thoughts, sensations, and feelings in order to connect to a truth greater than ourselves. – Fr. Richard Rohr

Building deep awareness, meditation is a mind body medicine that has been around for thousands of years. Different forms of meditation and contemplation exist, most have the same goal, to become well. Benefits of meditation include concertation, relaxation, inner peace, stress reduction, and emotional wellbeing. Meditation also alleviates chronic pain and health conditions in some individuals. Studies on meditation in the US can be traced back to the 1960s when researchers explored the health benefits of meditation. The study population included people who practiced transcendental meditation. Over time, this study found that just 10 to 20 minutes of meditation twice a day decreased metabolism, decreased heart rate, decreased respiratory rate, and slowed brain waves. It also reduced chronic pain, insomnia, anxiety, hostility, depression, premenstrual syndrome, and infertility. Patients with HIV and cancer benefited from meditation as well. The major finding from this and other studies is that meditation promotes a relaxation response, which is effective in treating diseases and maladies caused by stress.[43]

Spiritual gurus recommend following these practices as you begin the contemplative journey toward your inner and higher being using contemplation and meditation. These practices can be done together or as individual steps. Here is a list of practices you can follow to restore consciousness.

Prioritize contemplation- make time and space for the act.

Contemplate with purpose- contemplate a goal, past event, current challenge, past or future event. Examine what happened today. Reflect on the challenges you are experiencing in life. Consider solutions to the challenges you identified.

Relax- simply sit in silence

Pray or meditate- connect with God

Practice deep breathing

Evidence for Spirituality in Recovery

One of the most clear and tangible examples of evidence of the benefits of spirituality comes from the fields of recovery and addiction/ treatment. In a previous book I described examples of how spirituality helps individuals in their recovery. [44] Other researchers and authors have contributed evidence as well.

While the concept of spirituality in treatment program recovery from alcohol and drug use disorders is not new, it is real and there is evidence that spiritual wellbeing comes to many people in recovery. Researchers explored the evidence for spiritual foundations of recovery among treatment center clients. Clients identified faith or the need to believe in something that cannot be seen as a significant requirement for change and recovery. They report that one person said, ".... You have to believe in something. You can't have faith and not believe. You have faith to believe you can recover. You can't recover if you don't have faith that you can recover. That doesn't work. You have to have faith that you can recover."

Have you ever felt the beat of a drum, deep in your soul? Drumming has been viewed as a pathway toward healing, and a way to connect and build community. Some have told me that the drum is the heartbeat of the community or nation. Dan Dickerson is an American Indian Psychologist that developed Drum-Assisted Recovery Therapy for Native Americans (DARTNA).[45] Dickerson studied the effects of drumming with Native American patients with histories of substance use disorder. He also led focus groups to document perspectives from participants, providers, and the DARTNA advisory board. Results from his work show the positive effects of drumming on connecting the spirit, elevating one's mood, education, and strengthening community connections. Dickerson and colleagues write about one participant's experiences, "...I felt like I was equal in the spirit of everybody. They were taking time out of their lives, I was too, so we had consensus right there, and we're sitting around the drum and that's why the spirit works when we're all together."

There is also evidence that tapping on the 12 meridian points of the body can help relieve negative emotions and balance the energy system. Researchers call this the emotional freedom technique or EFT. To practice EFT, complete the following actions:

Emotional Freedom Technique and Scale

Identify the issue that is bothering you.

Determine the intensity of the issue on a 0 to 10 scale where 0 is the worst, 10 is the best.

Create a phrase to acknowledge the issue and accept your circumstances.

For example, "Even though I have a fear of losing my job, I deeply and completely accept myself."

Start the EFT tapping sequence based on 12 major meridians (side of hand, top of head, eyebrow, side of eye, under eye, under nose, chin, collarbone, under arm) and repeat the phrase three times, "Even though I ..... I deeply and completely accept myself ," while tapping on the meridian points. Repeat the tapping sequence at least two times.

Compare the intensity of the issue using the 0 to 10 scale, has the intensity of the issue decreased? Keep tapping until you reach 0.

Art

Do you love creating art? Art therapy, like it sounds, is the creating art. As therapy, art targets individuals with trauma, illness, and those seeking recovery. It can restore the sacred and the spirit. In my work I have witnessed the powerful impacts of art, giving someone a box of crayons and a big sheet of white paper, and asking them to draw something that represents how they are feeling. In other cases, I have witnessed the therapeutic effects of beading, sewing, painting, storytelling, videography, photography, medicinal plant preparation, embroidery, and drum making. All of these are various forms of art therapy. Researchers promote art therapy in treatment settings for its ability to promote emotional expression, encourage spiritual recovery, and illicit creative expression. Using principles of motivational interviewing and the stages of change, researchers asked clients to draw images of certain life events that brought them to treatment, for example, draw the crisis that brought you to treatment (this might be asked during the first session). Another art exercise is asking clients to draw a bridge of where they have been and where they want to be in relation to their recovery. A final example is to ask clients to create a cost-benefits collage that asks them to explore the costs and benefits of staying as they are or moving toward change and recovery.

Evidence for Spirituality in Art Workshops

I recently taught a workshop using an adapted form of art therapy. Here is a journal entry about this experience that I wrote on my flight home. Writing is a way that I process what is happening around me, and how I make sense of my interactions with the world and other spiritual beings.

I just finished a workshop with the California Rural Indian Health Board, Inc., Visual Cultural Models. What does visual – cultural – models mean? When I read the title, I felt the same way. What will we do with visuals, blended cultures, models, theories, ideas, and concepts? Like any task that feels unsurmountable, I thought about it for a few weeks and did nothing.

What am I willing to leave my home, family, and life behind for? Not much. The pressure mounts as I realize that the workshop must be the best it can be. Participants will travel from all over the state of California, leaving their loved ones and responsibilities behind. Anything less than "over the top" is a failure in my mind. Pressure builds. Feelings of not enough, not an artist, and this is going to be so lame are the lyrics playing in my relentless unconscious mind. But, like all well people, I reached out and asked for help. I am lucky because I am surrounded by creative people who have ideas, and we balance each other. I tend to land on extreme concepts that may be unattainable to execute, they bring me down to reality, and we meet in the middle. It was a Friday afternoon. A long week of staring at Zoom screens, budgets, Word documents, and PowerPoints zapped my creative energy. I called Jeanne Bowman and shared a few ideas about visual cultural models and what I would do… She's a professional illustrator.

I am a wannabe artist. Jeanne told me about her favorite author Lynda Barry.

Barry teaches adults to draw, many of whom left art and drawing in childhood because they were not perfect in art. We took this concept and developed a life-meaning exercise I could use in the workshop. We were intentional as we carved out the creative space for people to settle in. Seeing others' faces rather than the backs of their heads was absolutely necessary. We rearranged the table and chairs into a U shape, so everyone faced one another. We did some brief introductions, "Who are you and where do you work?" and then started a progressive story. I asked the group if anyone had heard of a progressive story... silence. Two photos were projected onto the screen, a girl in a car with a dog hanging out the side window and a line-up of traditional dancers in ribbon skirts. Every person was instructed to create a sentence that builds on the previous, similar to the game of I am going on a trip or telephone. I started... "Jane just got her driver's license and is taking Zoe, the dog, to the park." Next participant..." Zoe jumped out of the window to chase a squirrel." The story ended after about 15 people added creative ideas to the storyline. It ended with the squirrel throwing nuts at Zoe and Jane and driving off; the squirrel went home. The end. The progressive story worked because it required presence. We listened intently to the storyline and considered what we would add. We laughed and connected just 5 minutes into the workshop. So far, this experience was something I would definitely leave my home for. Next, we started the creative process. This is where things get a bit dicey because it's not easy to take people from telling a story about Zoe, the dog, into a creative space where they are bearing their heart, soul, mind, and legacy to a room of strangers. But the meetings with Jeanne, the illustrator, paid off, and we had some practice examples. Draw a mouse, step by step. Draw a human, step by step. I thought this process would take 5 minutes. It took at least 30 and some people were not done at the end of our three-hour workshop. They had difficulty getting into the creative flow, and there is no judgment; this is just the space they occupied. Next, we started the first actual drawing exercise. Draw four squares on a large piece of paper. You may fold the paper in half and then in half again (lines without lines). After you complete this task, create headers in each square.

Who are you?

What is the most significant event in your life?

How did you get to where you are today?

What legacy do you want to leave?

We worked on these four steps for quite some time, about two hours. But we were not in a space bound by time. When one of the facilitators told me it was time for a break pointing at her watch, I smiled and said, "People can leave any time. This is all a break." She smiled back. I could see people start to relax. This was a safe space.

I can be who I am. I can share what I think and feel. I can be grateful for this time.

The end exceeded my wildest expectations, seriously. People shared from their hearts. Tears were shed. Healing happened. Intentions for the future were set or at least illustrated. This process made people feel relaxed, grounded, and grateful. As we ended our time together, we reflected on what the experience meant and how to apply it to our lives and professions. People are more than just their physical and professional identities, the letters behind their names, titles, and expensive clothes.

It is human nature to compare ourselves to others, resulting in feelings of inadequacy and discontentment. But art changes that. People connect their hearts and minds to their experiences and history. Often, drawings represent memories of an experience an individual had (loss, birth, death, struggle) in the past. Sometimes, people have never talked about or written them down; they are buried beneath addiction, guilt, denial, and disease. These show up as powerful drawings and images that present a visual story of a person's soul experience. In these spaces, there is not much ego; in contrast, it is quite humbling.

Going Deeper: Takeaways for Becoming an Artist in Your Work and Life... for healing and the spirit. Ask for help; find creative people, trustworthy people. Share your ideas with them, get support, grounding, and out of your mind. Get into art. Seriously. I am always amazed at how many students, adults, and people talk about loving and leaving art. Life events happened. They feel they are missing time and the creative space. It's time to come back into the creative circle.

Art is a language of the soul. It conveys meaning and messages that words never will.

This was entirely worth leaving home. And I feel grateful and empowered by the stories that will be ingrained in my memory for a long time because they were conveyed with visual illustrations and feelings not found in our busy reporting, academic, and evaluating world.

Evidence for Mindfulness

Jon Kabat-Zinn is one of the founders of the mindfulness movement in the US and defines mindfulness as paying attention on purpose, in the present moment and, non-judgmentally, to the unfolding of experience moment to moment. I was first exposed to the concept of mindfulness in 2011, I had a long commute and was always searching for YouTube recordings that would feed my soul and ground me in some way. It was around this time that I really started walking a healing path, or being intentional about my thoughts, my emotions, and my practice. We know from research that mindfulness is linked to spiritual wellbeing and personal growth. People who practice mindfulness are spiritually grounded, well, and in some cases further ahead than people who do not practice mindfulness. Like many other interventions for healing, researchers explored mindfulness-oriented recovery enhancement for chronic pain and prescription opioid misuse in a randomized control trial (RCT). They randomized 115 patients with chronic pain into a treatment and control group 47 and assessed outcomes at pre and post treatment, and three months after the intervention. They explored changes in opioid use status and desire for opioids, stress, nonreactivity, and reappraisal. Researchers found that mindfulness is an effective approach and treatment for addressing co-occurring prescription opioid misuse, stress, and chronic pain. Mindfulness practices help us remember that we are not just spiritual beings or physical beings. We are integrated into a whole person by many facets of human and egoic form. Integrated approaches that incorporate aspects of spirituality with other healing modalities to treat spiritual deficits or unwellness are common. Integrative approaches are viewed as more effective than stand-alone approaches because they are woven into multiple levels, spaces, and places of being. Some examples of integrative approaches you might find on the path of mindfulness, healing, or spiritual wellness include cognitive behavioral therapies, peer recovery support, mindfulness, dialectical behavior therapy, trauma treatment, wellness treatments, and family works. Wellness strategies often include exercise, sleep hygiene, prayer, meditation, nutrition, and mind-body techniques. Family efforts may include education, groups, family therapy, and specific interventions when appropriate. Combined, mindfulness, contemplation, art, integration, and just paying attention to one's thoughts and the present moment is a way to ground oneself in the present, practice gratitude for what is available and experienced, and pray for what is to come.

The best way to capture moments is to pay attention. This is how we cultivate mindfulness. Mindfulness means being awake. It means knowing what you are doing. - John Kabat-Zinn

Evidence and Theories

Researchers, doctors, and therapists love to use theories to support the evidence base for the spiritual realm and spiritual wellbeing, among other things. Most spiritual theories come from the fields of theology and psychology. Over the years, there have been so many theories and theories are words, put into action, and then tested. What we think will happen if we do something specific or do not do something. They are not instructive, and they do not teach me how to be a spiritual human being. I can read about a theory and love it, align with it, but not internalize it or apply it to my life or circumstance. Maslow's Hierarchy of Needs came from his work on the Blackfeet Reservation in Alberta, Canada in 1939.[48] Although most of his research and publications fail to recognize the Blackfeet teachings, these Indigenous knowledge systems and beliefways were foundational to creating Maslow's Hierarchy of Needs. Maslow interpreted the Blackfeet teachings as physiological needs, safety needs, love and belonging, esteem, and self-actualization. This was the highest level of actualization and spiritual realization. In contrast, the Blackfeet teachings situate self-actualization at the beginning, followed by community actualization, and cultural perpetuity. Here Maslow's belief was that individual needs are priorities over community, this was the opposite of what the Blackfeet Tribe believed, that community or collective wellbeing is what matters the most. Wellbeing is conceptualized in different ways and with theories (the PERMA theory is just one).

Here wellness is based on Positive Emotion, Engagement, Relationships, Meaning, and Achievement.

What are some positive emotions that you experience?

What are you pursuing in your life right now?

Describe the relationships that you have, do they support your wellbeing?

Does your work/service make you feel like you are part of something bigger than yourself?

What are you doing right now?

How does this lead you to an accomplishment that you desire, now or in the near future?

Professors, researchers, and scientists are not the only people who can benefit from theories. Theories can be used by readers just like you to understand how evidence is created...how truth and knowledge is established in the vast world of spiritual wellbeing literature. While I was getting my doctoral degree, I went to a psychiatrist. I did not feel smart enough, fast enough, good enough to be in the program. I thought that I had an attention deficit, everyone did at that time. And I went to him seeking pills for my disease. To cure my wild and constant thoughts, so I could just concentrate for a few years on research, teaching, and learning. I thought it would be a lot harder to get diagnosed than it was. My psychiatrist was using theories and his clinical training (informed by theories) to give me a diagnosis of ADHD. He sat behind a huge executive desk, wire rimmed glass, slight build, perhaps the nuttiest person in Hillsborough, NC. His degrees, hunting photos, books, lined the shelves. Everything was in perfect order. He was the doctor; I was his patient. He had control, I had none. He gave me a diagnosis, based on theory and practice. I could be given medicine that would treat my disease. I went back to him every couple of weeks for a refill and a random urine analysis. Sometimes they would ask me to pee in a cup, to see if I was selling the drugs. At one point, I asked him, "How long do I have to take these meds? Will I eventually get better?" He looked at me like I was an alien and said, "You can take them forever, you will not get better. Most people just learn to deal with their attention issues." After I completed my degree, one of the first things I did was quit the meds. Not cold turkey–it was a phased process of letting go of the meds that made me think I could fly.

When I think about this story, I don't see my spirit. Where was my spirit that is writing today...telling the psychiatrist, "She must practice mediation, pray, reconnect...there is nothing wrong with you?"

Evidence and the Wheel of Wellness

Some theories and models are more complementary to a spiritual worldview and dimension. Consider the Wheel of Wellness developed by Meyers and others. Within this model, spirituality is at the center. Why wouldn't it be? Jill was 16 when she started seeing a psychologist for her depression and anxiety. It was getting to be too much, interfering with daily life, and making it nearly impossible to attend school regularly. Her grades were suffering. She was suffering. Jill came back from the psychologist one day and posted this Wheel of Wellness on her wall with a brown plastic thumbtack. It was just printed on an 8 ½ by 11 sheet of printer paper, but that wheel made a difference. She would look at the wheel, reflect on what she had done in each of the wellness domains to be well that day, and what she needed to work on.

This paper stayed hanging on her wall for several years, and it helped...

Indivisible Self

Researchers and theorists adapt models to create others, in this case, the Indivisible Self evidence-based model. Within this model the indivisible self is the "spirit." It is influenced by local, institutional, global, and life course events and conditions. Here there are five selves: the creative self, coping self, social self, essential self, and physical self. At any given time, these "selves" are interacting or influencing one another. Our various selves create multiple identities, multiple ways of showing up and being in the physical world.

Reflect on your Five Selves and think about how these selves show up in your life? When and how are you a creative person? What about coping? Consider the last time you had to endure or cope with a situation that was difficult. What did you practice? How about the social self? The last time you were at a party, at church? Who is the essential self or the essence of who you really are? When did you last practice and feel your physical self? Holding this book or listening to the words with your ears. Describe your Five Selves by closing your eyes and focusing on each question for at least 30 minutes. What image comes to mind? Write your responses below.

Who is the creative self?

Who is the coping self?

Who is the social self?

Who is the essential self?

Who is the physical self?

Evidence for Happiness

Are awakened people happier? I don't know. But I am amazed and cannot keep up with the stream of publications and journals highlighting all of the good work of academicians and possibly Artificial Intelligence (AI) in the field of happiness right now. The Journal of Happiness Studies has a collection of more than 1800 articles available related to happiness studies covering economics, quality of life, social sciences, and philosophy. The sheer number of published articles demonstrates interest and longing for happiness in the world, at all levels from academics to community members. We are living in a vibrant world with life happening all around us and in us. Our life experiences can bring us happiness, joy, and purpose. But many people are unhappy, without joy, and lack meaning and purpose. These people may feel spiritually unwell.

How can you tell if people are happy?

What is the measure?

This is a question for psychometricians, researchers, and the like. I, for one, cannot tell if people are happy. There are fake happy people in the world. They live with a fake happiness mask pasted on their face like a thick, orange-tinted foundation from the Wet and Wild makeup line. Luckily, I am not in charge of the World Happiness Study, a group of academics from Oxford, Columbia, Liverpool, and other prestigious universities are. I just learned about this study, but it has been going on for over ten years when the United Nations adopted a resolution claiming March 20 as International Day of Happiness. A country's overall happiness is a measure of its success, according to the United Nations and those in the know. Happiness is measured by life evaluations from the Gallup World Poll. Respondents are asked to imagine a ladder with the best possible life where 10 is the highest score possible and 0 is the worst. Respondents rank their current lives and responses are tallied up by researchers where countries rank from #1 to #137. Any idea on which states rank the highest or lowest? I did not. I knew, however that the happiness award was not going to the US. Results from the 2020 to 2022 study places Finland at #1 (7.8 out of 10) and Afghanistan #137 or last (1.8 out of 10). The US ranked #15 with an average score of 6.8 out of 10.49 With these rankings in mind, do you feel better about assessing your own happiness and that of the world around you? I do not. And, while the scores might be helpful for countries, what does happiness mean and how is it represented beyond satisfaction with life? What are the conditions and experiences that give people their best possible life in Finland and why are these conditions not present in Afghanistan?

What do people need to experience happiness?

Why is happiness viewed as an external experience separate from one's spiritual existence?

Lottery Winners and Happiness

Training for a half marathon on an indoor treadmill is a daunting task. Thank God for gym TV. The reality TV show, My Lottery Dream Home matches lottery winners with a realtor who finds them a dream home. Some winnings are modest, just $50,000 and others in the millions. After a few houses, the winners pick their homes. The last few minutes of the show is the family and friends having a grand time in their new homes, celebrating, laughing, and eating. How happy are they now? They seem beyond exuberant and beyond happy. But researchers have studied lottery winners and found that coming into large sums of money causes wealth shock, and has unanticipated negative consequences, often causing greater unhappiness.

Would winning the lottery make you happy?

What would change in your life today if you won the lottery? Physically? Spiritually?

Happy Thoughts Happy Life

If you are lucky enough to go to Harvard, you might know that the Psychology of Happiness class is and has been the most popular for decades. Bringing in scholars and students from all disciplines, there is a joint quest and seeking for what it takes to be happy. Afterall, isn't that the meaning of life to live fully and experience happiness and joy? How do we find happiness, and what theories support the concept of happiness? I am still looking. Fredrickson's Theory of Positive Emotions started the happiness quest in 1988, and it has gained momentum since then. Up until 1988, the clinical, treatment, and theoretical world was based on negative emotions and deficits. Fredrickson studied what happens when people experience positive emotions and found that positive emotions can undo negative emotions and protect wellbeing. Let's use the example of meditation. People who mediate may experience positive emotions like love, joy, and contentment. This positive emotion can broaden their positive feelings and thoughts towards themselves and others. Over time, positive emotions can build personal resources that promote wellbeing and increase life satisfaction, consciousness, and wellbeing.50 Focusing on negative emotions actually makes them worse. Our society, and the systems within, are obsessed with deficits, disparities, inequalities, and gaps. We are good at pointing out what is wrong. But what is right? What is right is focusing on the positive. Practicing gratitude, finding joy, practicing hope, being mindful, loving others. These are all positive emotions that we can experience in our lives, that actually enhance our wellbeing.

> When was the last time that you experienced awe, joy, or gratitude?
>
> What were you doing when you felt these emotions?
>
> Who were you with?
>
> Why did you feel these emotions?
>
> How can you have these experiences more often?
>
> Remember it is in focusing on the positive that gets us into a place of wellness, groundedness, connectedness, and union with the Creator.

No Separation, Just Evidence

Evidence tends to separate people and experiences into boxes. Imagine the PhD with 100 published research papers and lab running various clinical experiments on the evidence for spiritual wellbeing and the spiritual realm. Now consider the Tarot Card reader at the local fair, a booth hidden on the side with deep red and purple velvet curtains, cards and a mystical ball sits on the table. These are two vastly different spiritual seekers, but they are both seeking. And it is in seeking that we find a deep knowing about our existence as spiritual beings. Some might argue that the Tarot Card reader is all wrong. Others might tell us the PhD, or the pastor is wrong, all wrong, in their quest for evidence of the spiritual realm. I cannot tell you what to believe about the evidence for a spiritual life and that the spiritual realm exists. Only you can do that. But there is something we must recognize on the path of seeking evidence, and that is experience is the greatest teacher, and deep knowing that comes from these experiences.

Going Deeper: Evidence of the spiritual realm is everywhere. But we cannot access the powers and peace that come from the spiritual realm if we are caught up in proving or disproving that it exists. The spiritual realm comes to us when we are grounded in spiritual truths and see the beauty in all creation. Everything is a gift, including this moment.

Resources

Double-Slit Experiment, https://www.ourwonderlife.com/science-spirituality/

George Washington School of Medicine and Health Sciences, Institute for Spirituality and Health (GWish), https://gwish.smhs.gwu.edu/

Jon Kabat-Zinn, https://jonkabat-zinn.com

Reflections for Going Deeper

Read. What did you read that relates to the evidence you have experienced or observed?

Reflect. In what ways might you use art, drumming, EFT, and mindfulness to live a more purposeful, awakened life?

Remember. What can you remember that matters to you?

Abide. What do you accept?

4 Awakened Through the Life Course

———

What is Real?

The concept of God and rebirth and awakening are real. Not everyone believes that God is real, but without God (called by many other names), it feels like nothing is real. This chapter addresses the urgency to wake up and experience the second half of life or finding one's true self and soul. At the core of this urgency, and at times frustration, is the acceptance that not every human being is a conscious, awake human being. Their ability to experience consciousness, their highest self, is challenged by the fact that they have not embraced the concept of the spiritual rather than form-based existence. The belief in God gives us purpose, the deep knowing that we are created as spiritual beings to do specific work on this Earth. The reality of God, what we believe to be true about God, is the anchor for our lives. But many people today are walking down a path of truth that says, "I have my truth, you have your truth." This makes people separate from one another and from a collective purpose. This contributes to the spiritual crisis and non-awakening status of many human beings on the planet.

This chapter addresses the problem of what happens when people never realize that they are spiritual beings. In this chapter, you will read about awakening throughout the life course and how to recognize the stages of spiritual transformation when they occur. While these may look different for every person, there are common themes that we know to be true based on decades of research and personal narratives of healing and awakening. While much of what we know about awakening comes from the fields of recovery, psychotherapy, and Western behavioral health models, there is a lot we can learn based on various teachers that show up in our lives and throughout our life course. These teachers may be complete strangers, our children, deep suffering, or spiritual beings showing up in a human form. This chapter will expand your awareness about awakening and reaching your highest and fullest potential as a spiritual being. Because I embrace multiple identities (see Chapter 1), I find myself in everyday situations that teach me about the awakening process. These stories, based on human and spiritual experiences, make up the basis for this chapter and these teachings on awakening.

Stories are lessons from the soul. We live them, share them, and teach them to lessen the suffering of others.

Middle school can be a difficult time in life, with major transitions happening physically, emotionally, and intellectually. Kids can be unkind to themselves and one another. Talking with my middle school-aged daughter, I have heard the horror of what happens in the school hallways, the conversations teachers never hear, and the ways that kids manage and cope with this often-chaotic environment. As a parent I want my daughter to love her peers, even when they are being unkind. One particular student bullied her for three years of school, said unkind things, put her in a headlock, hit her, and not been a good conscious human. When this first started happening, I went to her school and reacted somewhat poorly. I stormed in one morning without a shower, my hair a mess, and asked to speak with the dean of students. She appeared several minutes later looking me up and down. I am sure that she thought This parent is completely out of her mind. I told the dean of students about the bullying, demanded that she do something about it immediately, and mentioned if she did not address the issue, I would take it to the superintendent. I left the school and that was the last conversation I had with the dean of students. It's been a few years. I see the dean in our community, I think loving thoughts about her, and how she was doing the best that she could do at that time. Even though it was completely pathetic and so very lame. This story, and many others, are signs that as a conscious awakened human, I fall into the trap of reacting, ego, and unkindness regularly.

Over the years, I asked my daughter why she thought that this student was bullying her. She said she didn't know. We talked about his home life, his inability to be kind, and his need to act out in physical ways that hurt others. I did not want to diminish the emotional and physical hurt that she experienced, but it was important for me to teach her about kindness and the golden rule. I told her that he was doing the very best that he could do, during those times at school when he bullied her. She looked at me and did not say anything, just a blank stare... Can you think of a situation where you reacted as an unconscious human when something happened to your loved one or child that was hurtful, unfair, or unkind? Did you face the situation head on, react, and demand punishment or retribution... or did you consider stepping back and taking it all in.

What am I seeing right now?

How am I feeling at the very core of my being?

What can I do to make this situation better without reacting in a physical, egoic way?

Is your reaction fueled by the need to be right, seen, and known? Or does it come from a place of love, understanding, and acceptance?

Because I am working on becoming more conscious and awakened to my highest self, I relapse into unconscious humanity most days. This should not come as a surprise to you, and if you are honest with yourself, you probably do as well. They tell us in recovery that relapse is part of recovery from alcohol and drugs. I know this to be true at a deeply personal and professional level. Here is a simple example of relapsing into unconscious and unawakened behaviors from a simple phone call. What am I seeing right now? I am seeing my phone screen tell me I have been on hold for 46 minutes. I am seeing life pass me by and thinking about all of the things I could be doing with these 46 minutes, besides waiting on hold for a live customer service representative to help me with the overcharges to my cell phone account. I finally had a human pick up the phone on the other end. We go back and forth about the problem of charges, lameness of all things. I rant and rave on and on for a while. They are thieves, stealing my money. It's against the law. I have other unawakened embarrassing statements that I cannot recall now. After each horrible and unconscious statement to the human representative on the other line, all I hear is... "Wow." He must have said wow at least 20 times on that call. Looking back, the word wow can mean so many things and I've used it when I feel a mix of emotions and wild and raging thoughts that cannot be contained by deep breathing, visualization, or other self-regulation techniques. How am I feeling at the very core of my being during the call? At the core of my being, I feel uneasy, tense, distracted, and frustrated. My mind is creating thoughts about these people, why they cannot just pick up the phone and have enough people at the call center to answer calls in a timely fashion. When the human on the other end finally answers, I feel relieved. Someone will hear my story and help me in some way, I hope. What can I do to make this situation better without reacting in a physical, egoic way? I could have stopped the thoughts, put on some relaxing music, and gone for a walk in the forest while waiting on the line (assuming there was cell reception). I could have remembered that the human on the other end was a spiritual being–not a tired phone service rep for a cell company who does not like his job but is doing the best that he can to provide for his family in a third-world country where incomes are well below the poverty level and any quality standard of living. What is fueling your reaction? Is it fueled by the need to be right, seen, and known?

Or does it come from a place of love, understanding, and acceptance? Initially, my reaction was all about being right, getting payment for money owed, making sure that the company knew they made a mistake, and getting them to pay for it. It did not come from a place of love, understanding, acceptance, or anything righteous. It was purely egoic, form-based, unawakened behavior. This is a simple story of me being unconscious and unkind to fellow humans. My mind was off the rails. I can always see this after an unconscious relapse, but I still fall from grace, into the pit of the egoic self. There is so much we know about being awakened from our personal experiences, walking with awakened people, and the company we keep. Drawing on the social identities we explored in Chapter 1, who we are, how we live, and our ability to tap into an awakened consciousness begins with who we think we are and what we think about ourselves, our purpose, and our divine nature. While all of us are called, chosen, and spiritual beings, the layers of trauma, victimization, loss, and abuse make some feel they are unworthy, unlovable by God, and damned to an eternal life of suffering. Stepping out of this narrative is possible...and group therapy, mentoring programs, mindfulness, 12-step models, and spirit-based activities can show us the way.

Waking Up Through the Life Course

Waking up, becoming conscious, involves shedding of the ego. Researchers and scholars have documented the awakening process at various stages of the life course. For example, Erikson's stages of psychosocial development lay out the stages of development and the human quest toward spirituality. Professionals use this model to make sense of developmental time points that correspond with the formation of identity, ego, and spiritual awakening. Success at each stage leads toward the path of an awakened self, failure in these areas takes people away from the awakened self.

Hinduism teaches us about the four stages of life. These are the student, the householder, the forest dweller, and the wise and enlightened person. Fr. Richard Rohr explains the four stages of life. Fr. Richard Rohr describes the first half of life and the second half of life. First half of life: We build a strong container to live in, we seek people to support us, we worry about what we will do, who we will marry, how we will support ourselves, and if our lives matter. We are consumed with form-based identities and materialistic worldviews. Second half of life: We identify with God and experience a universal or one consciousness. Some call this Christ consciousness. In the second half of life. we become our truest selves, we see the ego or false self for what it is, and realize we are not our egos. In the second half of life, we get ready for the transition from the physical and form-based existence to a spiritual one.

Erikson's model includes eight stages of developmental awakening based on one's age and I would add cognitive/brain-based abilities.[51]

Consider applying these stages to your own life.

Stage 1. Trust vs. Mistrust.

Feeding. In infancy, birth to 18 months, children begin to trust their caregivers who provide reliability, care, and affection. When caregivers fail to offer these things, children grow up unattached and mistrusting.

Stage 2. Autonomy vs. Shame and Doubt

Toilet training. In early childhood, when 2 to 3 years old, children experience autonomy vs shame and doubt. Consider potty training your child, in this process, children develop a sense of personal control over their physical bodies, and this creates a sense of independence. At the same time, when children are not successful in what they are physically trying to achieve, this creates a sense of shame and doubt.

Stage 3. Initiative vs. Guilt

Exploration. In preschool, children 3 to 5 years old begin to take control and exert power over their environment and explore new things. When they are successful, they feel a sense of purpose. But when children exert too much power and control, they are met with disapproval from their peers, which leads to a sense of guilt.

Stage 4 Industry vs. Inferiority

School-age children 6 to 11 years old, become part of the Western educational system where coping with the social and academic demands may challenge them. When they are successful in school, they feel competent; when they are not successful, they feel inferior.

Stage 5. Identity vs. Role Confusion

Social relationships. Adolescence, or ages 12 to 18 years old, is a critical time in the identity formation process. Teens develop a sense of self and personal identity.

Stage 6. Intimacy vs. Isolation

Relationships. Young adulthood, ages 19 to 40 years old, is all about forming intimate relationships with other people. When individuals have healthy relationships, they feel successful, and unhealthy relationships lead to feelings of loneliness and failure.

Stage 7. Generativity vs. Stagnation

Work and parenthood. Middle adulthood, ages 40 to 65 years old, is when people begin to think about their legacy and how they want to live. This might look like having children or doing work that has a positive impact on others. Success in this area leads to feelings of usefulness and purpose. Failure looks like shallow relationships and limited connections in the world.

Stage 8. Ego Integrity vs. Despair

Reflecting on life. Maturity, ages 65 until the end, is a critical time in the awakening process where many people look back on their lives feeling wise, connected, and fulfilled. Failure at this stage in life feels like bitterness, hopelessness, and despair.

The most important stage in this model is the last one, what Erickson called ego integrity. This is where an individual experiences emotional integration, acceptance of past life, feelings of happiness from the past, and having a love of humankind more than of the self. During this final stage, individuals achieve a spiritual sense that eliminates their fear of death. But we do not need to wait until the end of our lives to experience awakening.

How Awakening Happens

In my professional life right now (egoic and form- based), I am co-authoring a resource about problematic sexual behavior and sexual abuse. I realize this is a heavy topic and even reading these terms might be triggering to some. Our goal is to prevent abuse and respond to abuse in an effective manner that heals the victim, perpetrator, and family. But preventing this kind of abuse is challenging because there are so many different layers of dysfunction that go with sexual abuse, especially among children and or family members. Researchers and knowledge keepers often talk about adverse childhood experiences (ACEs) and trauma. We have documented how ACEs lead to chronic disease, depression, tobacco use, alcohol and drug use, obesity, and nearly every other physical health condition that you can imagine. But we know less about the healing experiences that come after the trauma. And by healing experiences, I mean healing the spirit and awakening toward consciousness.

One thing I learned from writing the Spiritual Healing book in 2023 was that healing is not a one-time event.[52] We do not become healed, and we are never truly healed as physical beings here on Earth. I actually did not realize this early in the writing process. I thought that healing was possible. People recover every day, and they are getting better from all things. Spiritual, physical, mental, and emotional. But life continues to happen. We experience loss, trauma, devastation, and disappointment, so the need for healing begins again. One of my favorite definitions of the word healing is positive change. Just positive change, that is it.

The goal of awakening the spirit is similar to how recovery and relapse are viewed. Here longer periods of time occur between relapse and recovery, and eventually, an individual no longer relapses; it's been 2 weeks, 6 months, 1 year, 3 years... since I used. In the space of being sober, we often find our spirits and a connection to God. You might have heard the term; they hit rock bottom. This might be for addiction or anything... meaning things could not get any worse. They are in the dark pit of hell on Earth, and they cannot go any further down; the only way out is to crawl out. One step at a time. It is in these steps that people might question what is happening, "Why me, God?" Or feel like God is not real, nothing is real, because the suffering is too much. Consider the parent who loses a child tragically in a car crash. It may take years or lifetimes to get over these kinds of losses, but it is possible. And when the shift occurs, when people begin to seek God out and see the universal connection of all things, they begin to truly heal and reach an awakened state.

Going Deeper: Trauma takes us to a spiritual place we often do not want to be. We don't want to feel the pain of loss, fear, shame, abandonment, and hurt at the soul level. Awakening is not an immediate experience during these times, at least not when we are going through them. But awakening does come. There is a purpose in suffering from adverse experiences or trauma. The way through the pain is in the pain.

Four Steps in Awakening the Spirit

Step 1. The beginning

Awakening often occurs through suffering. A tragic loss of some kind... a relationship ends, a child dies, and employment is terminated. Feelings like sadness, hopelessness, feeling lost, or emptiness often accompany suffering.

Step 2. Questioning

Suffering and loss make us question our foundational beliefs, the sacredness of life, our relationships, and connections, and at times the concept of God or a Creator of all things and Divine intervener.

Step 3. Looking within

When we feel that God has failed us, we often look within ourselves for the answers. This journey can be long and treacherous. It can also result in significant spiritual growth ending with a deep knowing that God is in us, and we are in God. All things are connected and working together.

Step 4. Awakening

Noticing, feeling, observing, knowing that we are spiritual beings is the goal of awakening. In this step of the journey, life looks and feels different. Individuals want to have purpose and meaning in their lives. They live out values that are connected to their highest self like generosity, love, forgiveness, non-attachment, and love.

Going Deeper: Because our lives are constantly in motion with different relationships and events happening, we will go through these steps many times. The goal is that each time a tragic loss or trauma occurs, we can step back and know what is happening to us, rely on our spiritual practices and a connection to God or a Divine being. Then, we can use these experiences to move to a higher level of understanding about our experience as spiritual beings having a human existence.

The Abandonment of Religion

GenX and GenZ are leaving organized religion in droves. Every generation of adults is becoming less religious than the generation that came before them. Generation Z is the least religious generation of all time with more than 37% being religiously unaffiliated.[19] While there are many possible explanations, the one that feels closest to the truth is that many religions have failed to teach and show people how to love like God loves. Religion has become a dualistic playground where blaming, shaming, judgment, and infantile behaviors are like a plague in the pews. Many preachers are at the pulpit for the wrong reasons...ego, fame, shame, and power. Some of the greatest successes of organized religion have also been their greatest downfalls. With the rise of technology and information that gives access to books, podcasts, sermons, and seminars, people are finding other ways to God. I was raised in the church and while it was not perfect, it was a place that grounded me in ways that still touch my DNA today.

Consider who your parents are or were.

What did they believe?

How did they live out these beliefs?

Did you attend church as a child?

What religious beliefs did your family embrace?

Children often become their parents. And children cannot choose their parents, siblings, or families. Parents have often already become something. They might be teachers, preachers, nurses, caregivers, lovers, and gardeners. But their life history stays with them. How they were raised, the traumas they experienced, and the blessings they were offered, all of this makes up who they are and how they show up in the world and to their children. One can easily see how dysfunctional cycles occur throughout generations, especially when left unresolved. However, in healthy and functional families, these cycles can be positive, promoting wellness and health.

There has been so much research on the spiritual benefits of peer mentoring and modeling that I cannot summarize it here or in an entire book. But I will tell you what we have learned in our work with elder-youth mentoring programs, peer mentoring programs, and peer models grounded in non-clinical, lived experiences...mentoring works. We implemented a 6-year peer recovery support program for individuals with substance use disorders. We collected qualitative data from more than 100 peers to learn more about their experiences and how spirituality was part of their awakening and sobriety process.

Peers talked about recovery as a spiritual process. Peers renewed their spiritual strength through meetings, prayer, smudging, and seeking out guidance when needed. Some felt the program reconnected them to their spirituality; one peer said, "I take a spiritual way on my sobriety, and I have the program to thank for that." Other peers talked about attending church and seeking out God has a higher power to teach them how to live. "If I stay accountable to my group members, myself, write (journal) meditate, pray, and exercise [I maintain my recovery]. Get involved in the community, meetings, and church." Others wrote, "I am seeking out a higher power God... to teach me how to live." [54]Remember spiritual awakening is all about your practice.

What is your practice?

How do you live?

Why does peer support and mentoring work so well to get people on the path of awakening? It works because it shows you how to live, the choices you need to make, the spiritual practices you can follow, how you must treat others... If you hang around spiritual gurus and conscious awakened people, you are likely to have some of this transferred to us. I tell my daughter to look around at the people she is hanging out with. These are the people that she is and will become. Being intentional about the company you keep is the first step toward awakening to the person that you want to be.

Make a list of the five people you spend the most time with.

Why do you hang around them? What do you get, and what do you give?

How do they react when things do not go as planned or when disappointment and bad things happen?

What are their spiritual practices?

Are there things that they do that make you think they are awakened or asleep?

Answers to these questions will put you on a path toward awakened relationships. Relationships that give you what you need to transform into the next dimension of spiritual wellness. Alternatively, if we stay in unhealthy, ungiving, and unbalanced relationships, it can be difficult. The main message that I hope I have conveyed in this chapter is that if you want to be awakened, be intentional about who you surround yourself with and the thoughts you tell yourself about who you are as a spiritual being connected to the universal Christ.

Observations of Spiritual Dimensions Based on Age and Place

Hospital birth wards and baby nurseries and nursing homes have a lot in common. They are both areas where a major physical and spiritual shift is happening. Babies are spiritual beings and just beginning their lives here on Earth. Most view the birth of a baby as a miracle, a gift from God, and loved, nurtured, and adored. Elderly people and others in nursing homes are spiritual beings as well, but they are often finishing out their physical life here on Earth. Elders often carry deep wisdom from their life experiences and have specific views about spirituality and or religion. I've heard many Elders tell me that they are ready to die. They are willing to transition into the next realm of being, which is called heaven for some. As you consider differences in spiritual wellbeing and awakening based on age and place, answer these questions:

> What does spiritual wellbeing and awakening look like in your life based on your life course, times, ages, people, and places?

> Where does awakening happen?

> How does awakening happen throughout the life course from physical birth to death?

Spiritual awakening may come from trauma or loss, and other spiritual experiences.

> How have you noticed this in your own life? Based on. Your age and place?

Why does age and place matter in the awakening process?

Church Camp and Awakening

Did you attend a church camp as a kid? Or even as an adult? Maybe you were a leader, on the work crew, an adult guest, or a counselor. If you did not attend a church camp, that is okay too. But for me, church camps were a place and opportunity for awakening as a young person growing up in Oregon. Church camps were an escape from the daily grind of living in a chaotic home, with sometimes limited food, and tense discussions, and unease. I could be anyone at a church camp, they did not know me based on my family or my home. Church camps invite non-believers to dedicate their lives to Christ, and believers to renew their vows, recommit their lives to Christ. In my experience, this process at camp looked like...

With our eyes closed and our heads bowed, raise your hand if you would like to invite Jesus into your heart as your personal savior and friend. Make a public profession of faith about what you want to believe and how you want to live your life. Or, come to the altar, pray with us if you accepted Jesus into your heart today. There are other invitations to non-believers becoming believers. For many, this begins a process of awakening early in the life course. It is a concept that existence is more than just the physical and form-based world. It is sacred, dynamic, connected, transcendent, existential, and metaphysical at times. My daughter just returned from church camp. Her friend accepted Jesus into her heart. She became a believer, attended the new believer meeting, received a Bible, and received lots of love from leaders and counselors. I don't know her full story, but I know pain when I see it. I prayed for this friend before she went to camp. I wanted her to know God in a way that was real, beyond the church pews. She found God at this camp. She has walked into the path of awakening. I will continue to pray for this friend and hope that she will continue the path of awakening in her life course. This decision will ground her and support her as she navigates young adulthood and makes decisions that will impact her future.

What Awakening Through the Life Course Looks Like

I cannot easily look at someone and tell you if they are awakened, but I can generally sit with someone for a few minutes, observe what they are talking about and pay attention to, and make a really good guess about their awakened status. This is important because on the awakened path we want to surround ourselves with those who are walking on that path, who seek and trust a universal power guiding every part of physical life, the good, bad, and in-between. When people talk about money, themselves, and material goods, it is a dead giveaway. They have not found the path of awakening. They are focusing on the physical things of this world, and while many give us comfort and luxury, they are not the goal of an awakened life.

An awakened life throughout the life course looks like:

Stillness

Love

Acceptance

Daily renewal

Grace

Faith

Non-judgement

Forgiveness

Patience

Non-attachment

Purpose

Going Deeper: On the path toward awakened consciousness, we must forgive ourselves first. For those who believe in the biblical teachings on forgiveness, you might know that God forgives us, Ephesians 4:32, "Be kind to one another, tenderhearted, forgiving to one another, as God in Christ forgave you." If you follow the Catholic teachings, you might believe in the Sacrament of Penance and receiving forgiveness from a priest.

There is a lot of evidence about waking up (spiritually) in the second half of the life course. Erickson's model on psychosocial development and the ego calls this final phase integrity vs. despair.[51] During this shift from the first to second half of life, the hope is that most people will begin looking inward at their lives, see the Creator of the Universe and how the Creator had a hand in all of the life they lived, good, bad, and in-between experiences. It is a sad time when people transition and have not found peace in the lives they lived. I was talking with a hospice nurse about the second half of life. We talked about the difference in some patients who were transitioning in their final days. Those who had faith, peace, and spiritual integrity often transitioned without fighting death. However, individuals feeling despair, regret, and grudges had a hard time transitioning. She recounted how their faces would say it all during the last seconds of their lives. Some looked happy and peaceful, others shocked and in disbelief.

We also see differences in the first and second half of life from our recovery and treatment data. People who are older are more likely to complete treatment and recover than younger people. I believe this is because people who are older are heading into their second half of life. They realize that time on Earth is limited, they are living and have the disease of being human, they will die so it's time to get serious about what matters, about purpose, meaning, faith, and seeking out a God in the forest or in the hospital bed or at church or in the temple or sweat lodge.

John is in prison for the fourth time. Like many individuals in our nation who are incarcerated, he experienced early childhood trauma. His parents spent time in prison for drug related charges. Throughout his life he was exposed to drugs and alcohol and started using them as a coping mechanism at the age of 11. John is in the second half of life. How do I know this? It is by his work and his approach to all things. He has experienced deep loss, and at the same time, profound growth. He is active in ceremonial teachings, works with youth, and has a heart for all of Indian Country.

Jane is a one-dimensional human. She's only 21 so she has time to wake up, but the process of watching her single dimension is painful. She is driving everyone crazy. She is constantly concerned about herself, her looks, her job, her material wealth, and how she appears on the outside, without any attention to what is happening on the inside. This has taken a toll, with trips to the emergency room for overdoses and regular panic attacks.

I have had a hard time grappling with the concept that some people will never step into an awakened state. They will continue to suffer in the physical and spiritual realms. Buddhists and others believe in reincarnation–the process of coming back as another life form, after the physical death of this life. Based on my religious upbringing, I never thought that this was possible or true. I thought we had just one spirit, one life, that is all there is. But the more that I live, the more that I think anything is possible.

My research has taken me to some unforgettable places and people. For years, I worked with the Northern Cheyenne Tribe and stayed at the

Wild Rose Center. This non-profit dedicated to women and children was unassuming at the top of a dirt road and pasture with a couple of single wide mobile homes. Cows graze in the pasture and cars are always parked in the lot. A sweat lodge erected proudly in front of the homes and cows look on, waiting for something to happen. Sister Mary was a Franciscan nun that stayed there; she actually worked on the Northern Cheyenne Reservation with St. Labre School, a former Indian Boarding School in Ashland Montana serving Native youth and the community. The history of Indian Board schools is another story with entire books, libraries, and lawsuits written about it. The Catholic Church as an institution is awakening to its history and the impacts sexual abuse, violence, genocide, and forced removal of children had on the current history of civilization and the Indigenous peoples of North America. Even with this history, nuns, priests, and congregations still commit their lives to the Catholic religion. Mary was one of them, and over time, I got to know her. She was awakened. She taught me about Fr. Richard Rohr, mindfulness, prayer, and being deeply aware of the universal consciousness guiding our lives and extending into eternity. One night we were sitting in the living room and started talking about reincarnation. I asked Mary, "Do you believe in that?" She said, "Well I don't know why not. For all I know those cows out there are reincarnated. It's possible. Many people don't get it right the first time. They have to come back and try again, to live out the lives that God intended for them. To awaken." That was not the response I expected. I thought she would politely say, "No."

Alan is a Chinese healer. He is brilliant and quirky. He is an atheist and does not believe in God or any gods. I asked him, "What do you think about reincarnation?" He said, "Have you ever seen a 5-year-old music prodigy play Mozart?" I nodded and smiled.

Awakening and the 12 Steps

Becoming sober (from all things) and reclaiming what I have lost has awakened different parts of my spirit that I didn't know existed. Step 12, Having had a spiritual awakening as the result of these steps, we tried to carry this message to alcoholics and to practice these principles in all our affairs. But this message is for everyone, not just for "alcoholics." We can all have a spiritual awakening.

Some people and individuals with addiction diseases never get to the point of awakening. I've thought about this for a while. How come they suffer? Why are they not healed by medicine, treatment, therapy, or God? What a horrible, unloving God who watches people suffer, fall from grace, and ingest or overdose on substances that take away their spirit.

Eduardo Duran writes about being awakened, healing the spirit and soul wound in his writings, podcasts, and books.[55] We worked together at Northern Cheyenne on a veteran's suicide prevention program. I recall thinking that he was awakened, enlightened, and someone I wanted to sit next to without saying a word...it was the being piece that we covered earlier, being without words. He embraces a holistic and Indigenous worldview and has the ability to connect the physical to the spiritual unlike anyone I have met. Duran describes the early stages of healing, and the importance of staying with people who can protect you from relapse, or not walking on the healing path. He recommends these ten steps for healing and walking on a healing path. Pray every day for your spiritual health. Get up early and greet the morning sun with a prayer of thanksgiving. Leave an offering to the spirit of alcohol or other drugs. Also leave an offering to the spirit of recovery, wellness, and healing. Meditate for at least 10 minutes then do your morning routine, shower, etc. Breakfast should be healthy and eaten in a mindful way. Take your time and be grateful for each bite. Sometime during the day, you should do some physical exercise unless your work has plenty of it. Work should also be an act of gratitude and mindfulness.

Regardless of what you do for a living (of course it has to be something that is wholesome and does not hurt anyone). Sneak in a prayer every now and again if the task permits. During one of the days in the week you should set up ample time for yourself. This time can be used to see a counselor, sponsor, minister, holy person, or such. Once you spend time doing spiritual counseling work then you should have time just for yourself. Treat yourself with kindness and respect. With the proper motivation and intent do good things for others. These can be one-time activities or getting into a project that is going to help others. Dedicate your intent to the purpose that you want to reconcile with in order to restore balance with the natural order.

The time with your loved ones should be part of your day. If you have a family, try to prepare, and eat dinner with them. Read something that is good and do some other form of entertainment before sleep. As you approach sleep, be mindful of dreams and what these may be bringing to your life. Be ready to recall your dreams and commit to trying to understand their message. He encourages people to recognize that sobriety is part of living, and that we are also human. Sometimes we fall short of our goals, or we walk off the healing path. We must not linger. We must keep moving forward, forgive ourselves and others, and continue to walk in a healing and mindful way.

Part of awakening is ceremonial. A ceremony is a formal practice or series of practices that mark a specific path, toward purpose and transformation. I was interviewing another clinical psychologist yesterday. We were talking about trauma and PTSD among Vietnam veterans. He knew all of the Western clinical approaches to healing for them, the treatment they would need to get past the trauma. But when we talked about ceremonies, he elevated those as just as important as the clinical work. He shared, "One ceremony from the Lakota is Wiping the Soul. It is a ceremony that comes from the Lakota that was passed down. If you had killed someone, there was a purification ceremony for you. It was performed at night, in darkness. There are a lot of those kinds of things that are there, but these are not readily available in literature. It is passed down through word of mouth. You deal with a lot of it that was avoided, like at Wounded Knee. People were worried about the next massacre." There are many ceremonies that can help us awaken. But at the end of the day, it is up to each person. They choose the awakening process and often this comes from suffering. Awakening is somewhat undefined, not linear, and not generalizable. There are pointers that help you determine your level of spirituality or awakened consciousness, but these are just words and numbers. The spiritual realm is not defined by words, degrees, titles, and knowing. The spiritual realm is the interior practices of one's life. Their deepest ideas, memories, thoughts, and connections to the highest form of spirit, God (called by many other names).

Chosen

When you walk into my home, there is a big wooden sign I bought on Etsy, it reads, "You are chosen" 1 Peter 2:9. I look at this reminder at least 10 times a day, maybe more. It is a reminder that you are, and I am chosen. It is in the space of being and feeling chosen that we give ourselves permission to awaken to the blessings and gifts that God has intended for our lives.

No matter your position on awakened consciousness, you must think about the concept of being chosen, "Why me? Why am I awake when most of humanity is still sleeping?" Many cultures, religions, and faiths believe that they are the chosen one, and in some cases the only chosen ones. Many years ago, I managed a duplex and had a renter who was a Jehovah Witness. I did not know much about Jehovah's. Only that they knocked at many doors calling people to follow their ways. They believe that only a certain number of people are chosen and will be admitted to the eternal party and afterlife. I apologize for brevity here;

I am not a religious scholar or expert. But I recall thinking this was exclusionary, why would a loving God only select a few for eternal life?

A tribal cultural leader from Oklahoma was talking about his teachings and ways. He mentioned that early on, he thought only his tribe was the chosen tribe, that others were not chosen by the Creator. Mormons, with many amazing values, believe they are chosen. That people must be baptized in their temple, follow their ways, tithe, and live according to their teachings and principles. This is what it means to be chosen in their way of being. The Bible includes more than 25 verses about being chosen. Matthew 22:14, "For Many are called, but few are chosen." I've struggled with this because I think, Why me? Why not my neighbor down the road? Maybe they will be chosen or awakened later? Someone once told me that God chooses us, he already has, all of us. But it is we who need to choose God or the path of awakening. If you do not believe in God or the Bible, replace the word chosen with sacred. You are sacred. This is a reminder and blessing to remember.

Are you awakened? Where is the path you are on leading you? Are you excited about the destination or are you feeling despair, overwhelm, shame, and regret? These are the questions and answers you must consider as you walk with intention toward awakening. I do not know your answers, but you probably have an idea after reading this chapter. What I can say about the awakening process is that it does not occur overnight, and it is not defined by time. We are human, so we will inevitably fall from grace. But on the awakened path, we start to see more of the awakened traits in our lives. Love for everyone. Patience. Forgiveness for those who are unkind and unjust. Stillness. There are so many signs. Thomas Merten reminds us that the mystic or awakened conscious human is not the one who said, "Listen to what I've obtained, listen to what I've realized. The true awakened person says, "Look at what love has done to me." And, on the path toward awakening, we must remember that we are no better than those who are not awakened. The Divine walks behind us and in front of us. The ask is that we give love and presence to others.

There is confidence and peace on the awakened path, and I do hope that you will find it. That is the goal of this chapter and really this book. Why not be awakened?

Resources

Center for Action and Contemplation, https://cac.org

Erickson's Stages of Development https://www.ncbi.nlm.nih.gov/books/NBK556096/

The Trauma Therapist Project interviews Dr. Eduardo Duran on healing. https://www.thetraumatherapistproject.com/podcast/podcast/eduardo-duran-phd-healing-moral-injury

5-Year-Old Italian Music Savant Playing Mozart https://www.youtube.com/shorts/PMk_AYbmsxY

Reflections for Going Deeper

Read. What did you read that speaks to your own awakening experience?

Reflect. In what ways might you use these words to address your own healing?

Remember. What can you remember that matters to you?

Abide. What do you accept?

5 Developing Spiritual Roots

Acknowledging Your Roots

Depending on where you stand today, you might have spiritual roots planted based on your childhood or a grandmother or a local church and pastor. Over the years of working in recovery and being in recovery, I have come to know the importance of our environment and the social, emotional, physical, and mental conditions that impact our spirituality. This chapter addresses the problem of underdeveloped spiritual roots and how to develop spiritual roots that connect people to their highest awakened and conscious self. Much of my early research was exploring the social determinants of health. I wanted to find out what conditions contributed to early death in populations. From this research, I know things about our conditions.[56] The US ranks fourth in the world for people living with diabetes- 38.4 million people and it's a leading cause of death. What is it about diabetes that kills people? It is the conditions that they live in, the jobs that they have, and the access to healthy foods. Healthcare systems, preventative medical treatments, and generational factors lessen or increase deaths from diabetes, depending on what side of the tracks you are on. In fact, my research found that employment was the greatest predictor of deaths from diabetes among American Indians and Alaska Natives living in the Great Plains Region.[38] If someone has a job, they are less likely to die from diabetes than someone who does not have a job. What does it take to have a job? A well mind, body, and spirit. When we are unwell, it is difficult to work or care for ourselves, our spirit, and our loved ones.

He will be like a tree planted by the water that sends out its roots by the stream. – Jeremiah 17:8

One of the most powerful models used in recovery is called the Healing Forest Model.[58] I wrote about this in one of my previous books. White Bison and other social theorists created the concept of a healing forest. The Healing Forest model is based on the idea that if one tree in a forest is sick and removed, and brought back to health, then returned to a sick forest; the tree will become sick again. Healing communities require everyone's participation in the healing process. Moore and Coyhis advocate that this is the only way systemic change will occur. The roots of the forest must address anger, guilt, shame, and fear. The new roots must be based in culture and spirituality. The soil and conditions surrounding the forest must be healthy, vibrant, and nutrient-dense, feeding the roots so that every tree thrives.

This model and approach tell us that if we are living in a forest that is not well, we will remain unwell. If we want to develop spiritual roots, but the forest that we live in is sick, it's nearly impossible to do this. But most people do not try to change the forest. It is hard. It takes time. It takes a willingness to want a different life. For those on the path toward developing or strengthening their spiritual roots, the process is intentional and relentless. And it is worth it. But the problem with the Healing Forest Model and developing spiritual roots is that not everyone is born into a healthy forest. David Katerndahl studied the role of spiritual roots and health outcomes using the Spiritual Symptom Scale.[59] He found that lower spirituality scores (measured by 0 to 5) were associated with poorer mental health, overall health status, and feeling that your life lacks meaning. Here is an example of that scale. Answer the questions based on a response of '0' "none of the time" to '5' "all of the time".

Spiritual Symptom Scale

How often do you feel peaceful?

How often do you feel a reason for living?

How often do you feel your life has been productive?

How often do you feel a peace of mind?

How often do you feel a sense of purpose?

How often are you able to reach down deep into yourself for comfort?

How often do you feel a sense of harmony within yourself?

How would you respond to these statements.

Do you feel peaceful all of the time?

Do you feel your life has a sense of purpose?

The higher your score or agreement with these statements, the more deeply you have developed your spiritual roots. This, in turn, has all kinds of benefits to your physical, mental, emotional, and spiritual wellbeing.

Here is a story about my beginnings, my spiritual roots and forest.

I grew up in Christian home. This was the beginning of my spiritual roots. I never lived in a world where God did not exist. My forest consisted of a rural low-income house, a church on Sunday morning, evening, and Wednesday nights, and many kind Sunday school teachers. Music was a big part of my forest. I played the piano for the church, weddings, sermons, services, and more. It made me feel like I belonged in that place, that I had a purpose from God to do something with my life. I wish I would have known that God can be called by many other names. I wish that I felt more love from my family as a child and teenager. Love was conditional, if you do good we love you if you do bad we do not love you as much. Unconditional love and God is love was not always the message I heard. The forest I lived in was punitive, God is sending you to hell if you lie, cheat, steal... I was okay with this because I did not know a different God of the forest. I had times that I questioned what a loving God was doing when I lost loved ones, partners, and friends to disease or tragedy. Church camp were forests that developed my spiritual roots. I recall being in 4 or 5th grade at Camp Tadmor in the hills of the Willamette Valley in Oregon. Every summer I would attend the church camp, but I never had money for supplies like sleeping bags, a swimming suit, extra shoes, or the canteen. Church camp was where the kids showed up. Kids from materialistic worldview families and economic privilege. They would bring new sleeping bags, mini toothpaste and shampoo bottles, new clothes, swimsuits, and money for the canteen and camp t-shirts. When you lack money and you look poor and feel poor, it is hard to feel loved by a universal God. You are not concerned about God in this space and time, you are just concerned about what you are going to eat, or which kid is going to make fun of you because your clothes are too tight, and your shoes are the cheap ones that make you slide all over the basketball court. At Camp Tadmor, there was a call, every night... "Who wants to be saved?" Heads bowed and eyes closed, I peeked out of one eye to see who raised their hand or walked forward then out the door for mentoring with a pastor who would free them of their wicked sins. This was the narrative of the forest. It was not a bad narrative, it's just what it was. My forest today is a literal forest. At the end of a dirt road, I see God in the animals, the fox and mountain lion that live here. God is in the stars and the trees and the flow of Whychus Creek. It is a healing space for me. It is where I have locked in my spiritual roots and found the path toward awakening, my spiritual roots are deep, resilient, and expansive. My faith community is not perfect, but it can be helpful. Sermons always teach me about how to live and how to deal with what is going on in this wild world. I volunteer on a youth group committee and support various activities about developing spiritual roots in our young people in the community. This is a beautiful process and makes me know that I belong to the beloved Creator of the Universe. I am his and he is mine. I am intentional about my forest. I don't have many visitors (at my house or in my life). God is all I need. As you consider the process of deepening your spiritual roots. Consider these questions.

> What was the forest like that you grew up in? Physically and spiritually.

> Who was the forest or the tree that supported you?

> What do you wish that you knew as a young tree in the forest?

> What is your forest like now? Is it healing or damaging?

Your answers to these questions are the beginning of developing your spiritual roots and story. Considering where you have been in your life, and where you would like to go, as a spiritual person.

Forests are a powerful metaphor to extend our ways of knowing about connections, support, and caretakers. I was listening to a podcast by Suzanne Simard and her work on the Mother Tree Project.[60] This project is about finding new ways to protect the biodiversity and carbon storage of our forests as climate change impacts forest regeneration. Simard dedicated her life's work to exploring the forests, the intersection of life and history, and family within the forest. In every forest, there is a Mother Tree. The Mother Tree is the oldest tree with the most connected nodes in the forest. The Mother Tree shares excess carbon and nitrogen through networks that help seedlings or smaller trees survive. The Mother Tree communicates with the young seedlings around them and is connected to hundreds of other trees in the forests. Mother Trees can be both male and female. They create resilient and healthy forests, even after they pass on, they help maintain rich biodiversity.

Going Deeper: We can learn a great deal about healing and communication, final gifts, and offerings from the forests, and the Mother Tree. And our memories, genetic makeup, our relatives, and our decisions are so closely linked to the Mother Tree concept.

Who are our mother trees?

Where do they show up in our lives?

How did they come to us?

What carbon (or knowledge and wisdom) has been left for their offspring (children and families)?

Remember, light is not so much what you directly see as that by which you see everything else. -Fr. Richard Rohr

Lack of Roots, Pass Darkness on To Others

If you read the news, or the introduction of this book, you know our world is in crisis and many are unconscious, unawakened to their truest selves. We have suffering caused by unconscious people in positions of power. War, famine, drought, severe weather, gun violence, mass traumas... I could go on, but I will not. While these events seem external, on the physical realm with physical form-related consequences, they are in fact signs of a spiritual crisis. Our world is in a spiritual crisis, and this is evident in how people are living, the decisions they are making, and the lack of general awareness they have about others and the spiritual realm. Many are not rooted in any spiritual praxis, they are consumed by form...posting on social media, plastic surgeries, winning, anything that feeds the ego. The ego loves to make enemies and be offended, people are unknowingly led by their egos into situations, reactions, and spaces. And within the ego and these spaces, there is no spiritual purpose or connection to the divine purpose for our lives. All things are based on feeding the egoic self, bigger cars, winning higher stakes games, or conquering others.

I am the Light of the world. – Jesus of Nazareth

Individual vs. Collective Spiritual Roots

The lack of spiritual foundations is most obvious in the signs of individualistic thinking and being. Here there is no collective, the goal is for individuals to win and others to lose. David Brooks' book, The Second Mountain, explains why the shift from individual to collective living must happen.[61] And the benefits of that collective living run deep.

If you consider a line with individualism on one side and collectivism on the other, there are spaces between these extremes that you may identify with. Individualism tells us that you are the sum of your choices. Collectivism tells us that you are the products of your environment and social structures. Within these two extremes there are spaces, libertarian, liberal, utilitarian, and post postmodern. Individualism was influenced by the philosophy and teachings of people like John Locke and Carl Hume. Collectivism was influenced by the German philosopher and sociologist, Karl Marx.

> Individualism. Independent. Goal oriented. Competition. Private and self-knowledge. Direct communications.

> Collectivism. Related. Belonging. Duty. Harmony. Advice. Context.

Consider your sacred identity and the messages that you tell yourself about who you are.

Where do you fall on the line of individualism to collectivism?

How are you developing your spiritual roots?

What is your collective and sacred identity?

Who claims you in this process?

Developing spiritual roots requires a collective identity with God and a deep knowing that we are guided by a Divine presence and source in our lives. We have gone too far on the path of individualistic thinking. We must reframe and redirect our thinking and knowing toward a collective presence and belonging as spiritual beings. But not everyone is open to a collective way of living and in this collective body the ego does not have enough room to grow, conquer, and succeed.

We do not think ourselves into new ways of living, we live ourselves into new ways of thinking. - Fr. Richard Rohr

Signs That You May Lack Spiritual Awakening

Some people lack spiritual grounding and never fully awaken, they will not grow no matter what. Is this because God does not love them? They are going to reincarnate to learn the lesson again. They have not suffered enough. Here are some signs that you may lack spiritual grounding and connections:

No self-regulation

No coping

No love for others

No purpose

No collective identity

No hope

No considerations for other

No awareness

No consciousness

Parents have a big task. Bringing up children in a way that goes beyond the physical form and introducing the spiritual dimension of wellness in a world that is often polarized with mixed messages and a dualistic, egoic agenda. Many are waiting for some big shift to happen within the collective. This is happening in some places now. When we think about healing the spirit and consciousness rising, forgiveness is at the center of this. There is power in the human touch, healing that can come. Child soldiers have been a mainstay in recent African warfare. Child soldiers from Sierra Leone, Sudan, Uganda, Eritrea, and the Democratic Republic of Congo have written memoirs about their experiences of war.[62] I was told a story about these young African child soldiers. They did not know a kind human touch or how to be cared for, the love of a parent or relative. They endured many wars and traumas and finally came home. But they could not find solace, these boys were now young men. They were anxious, screaming, reliving the traumatic memories of war, genocide, and witnessing suffering. Villages could not help them; they tried everything to calm their spirits. One evening a group of grandmothers gathered to talk about these young men, and what they needed to heal. They decided that holding them in their arms was what these men needed, a loving embrace from a trusted grandmother. This worked. Just holding them and caring for them. My Elder and friend tells me about the Blackfeet teachings that are similar to this. They wrap babies up in oil and smother them with the human touch so that they know that they belong. Today, touch is overly sexualized. This is a problem.

Creating Boundaries for Spiritual Grounding and Development

Boundaries are necessary for individuals and communities as they strengthen spiritual foundations and become conscious and awakened beings. You may have personal experiences with this when your boundaries were violated. Maybe this involved a family member and their illness, or it could be something as simple as a colleague at work, who constantly oversteps and over asks - making you feel violated and uncomfortable. No matter what the situation, these tips will help you as you create healthy boundaries in all relationships.

Know what your boundaries are.

Understand co-dependence and what unhealthy, unkind, and unbalanced relationships look like.

Seek support from others in maintaining these boundaries.

Understand that boundaries are often violated through manipulation and addiction.

Provide support for loved ones without violating boundaries.

Restorative Justice Models That Heal the Forest

We've reviewed theories and some clinical approaches to restoring the sacred in previous chapters. We did not focus on models that heal the forest, so here are some approaches that show us that healing can happen. We have research and evidence that these models work. I first came across the concept of restorative justice while teaching an undergraduate health class. I had not considered it before, but a colleague sent me an article that outlined how an Alaska Native village in Alaska used restorative justice approaches to bring people back into the circle after being taken away and imprisoned for sexual abuse. Models can be ways to create spiritual roots, restore lost connections, or address family conditions that fail to grow strong spiritual roots. The Duluth Model is just one. Beginning in the 1980s, a small community in Minnesota demanded that domestic violence perpetrators keep victims safe and accountable.[63] Using a community approach this model promotes improved conditions addressed imbalances in power and control of the spirit and healed many. The Family Wellness Warriors Initiative from South Central Foundation in Alaska was designed to heal the forest and restore the sacred circle of life. Their philosophy was to embrace the entire family and include those who have been harmed and those who have harmed others using the strengths and spirit of Alaska Native people and communities. Their initiative was grounded in biblical teachings, "...To give unto them beauty for ashes, the oil of joy for mourning, the garment of praise for the spirit of heaviness, that they might be called trees of righteousness..." (Isaiah 61:3).

Going Deeper: When we develop our forest, care for our roots, and see that beauty can come from suffering, we are deepening our spiritual roots.

At the heart of these models is the concept of forgiveness and restoration. I am not one who can easily forgive, but I am working on it. Forgiveness looks like this narrative for me.

Forgiving a Friend

I will never forgive her because she broke my trust, said awful things about me, and placed my livelihood at risk.

A few years pass...

I will forgive her because she was acting at the level of consciousness that she embodied, her response could not be any different because this is just where she was at, at that time.

Forgiving a Perpetrator

The young man who sexually abused me. Years go by without a word. No one knows. Eventually more people will know. I hate him. I fear him. I hope he is dead.

Four decades pass...

40 years later I forgive him. He was acting at the level of consciousness that he had at that time. He could not do any better and he was acting out of his own desires with no self-regulation or control.

You see how forgiveness plays out. And this forgiveness is often found in the second half of life. It is not something we can easily embrace as young egoic and form-focused beings. At least for me. We have used the Heartland Forgiveness scale to assess forgiveness.

Consider how you might respond to these sample questions.[64] Answer the questions below based on a response of '0' "none of the time" to '5' "all of the time".

Forgiveness Scale

I continue to be mad at others who have hurt me.

I don't stop criticizing myself for negative things I've felt, thought, said, or done.

If others mistreat me, I continue to think badly of them.

It's really hard for me to accept negative situations that aren't anybody's fault.

The Gratitude Questionnaire is another example of how we can reflect on gratitude as a practice.[65] Consider how you might answer these sample questions. Answer the questions based on a response of '0' "none of the time" to '5' "all of the time".

Gratitude Scale

I have so much in life to be thankful for.

If I had to list everything that I felt grateful for, it would be a very long list.

I am grateful to a wide variety of people.

As I get older, I find myself more able to appreciate the people, events, and situations that have been part of my life.

The Vision: Creating A Healing Forest

What does a world look like that is spiritually grounded as much as it is physically rooted?

If we could see people's spirits, the face they were born with before they came to this Earth, we would change how we live and what we think about. We would have a better and different way of developing relationships with those who strengthen our spiritual roots. Families have an obligation to create the best forest that they can. It may not be perfect, but it can be what they have. Developing spiritual roots in families is often based on the beliefs, values, and worldview that they hold. For families that hold a biblical worldview, they may teach the Ten Commandments. Teachings may be through memorization, prayer, fellowship at a church, or small groups. Prayers at bedtime, words of grace and gratitude, showing love and kindness, acts of service and forgiveness. When parents model these values and practices in their own lives, their children see it and follow them. It is not what we say that matters but what we do and how we live that matters the most.

Individuals and families who are not religious can also practice deepening their spiritual roots. Begin with prayer and meditation. Find time to give back to the community that you live in through service and financial donations (if possible). Attend spiritual retreats, spiritual camps, yoga, meditation retreats, mindfulness retreats, spend time in nature, keep a gratitude journal, smile often, find people and places that feed your spiritual longing for consciousness and wellbeing. In a healing forest your spiritual identity and worldview is known. Your spiritual identity is the essence of who you are, it is clear to others and those who live in the forest with you and among you.

What does your family/forest look like?

Ask someone you trust to describe your essence (that is what you are without personality or form).

What evidence is there that your spiritual community (churches and faith-based organization) bears fruit from deep roots?

What is happening in your community that shows a deep spiritual presence of God and a connectedness to the creator that is not based on form?

As you begin to develop your spiritual roots these will spread like the hormones and chemicals from a mother tree, just like Suzanne Simard tells us. Others around you will notice that you have changed, that you are not as reactive, judgmental, or egoic. You might even notice the spiritual roots in others. You may be able to talk to their spirits, their consciousness with your own consciousness, and without words. This is when you know you are on the right path. Or the path that leads to spiritual wellbeing and wholeness. The path is windy, and it is not direct. There are times you will lose the path, but your roots will remain.

He is like a tree planted by streams of water, which yields its fruit in season and whose leaf does not wither. Whatever he does prospers.-Psalm 1:3

Resources

The Healing Forest: A Model for Community Wellbriety by White Bison,

http://peter.growinme.com/wp-content/uploads/Healing-Forest-Community.pdf

The Mother Tree Project by Suzanne Simard,

https://mothertreeproject.org/about-mother-trees-in-the-forest/

Reflection for Going Deeper

Read. What did you read that helps you see God?

Reflect. Who is in your forest? What do the roots look like? How do you deal with unhealthy trees?

Remember. What can you remember that matters to you?

Abide. What do you accept?

6 Making the Shift, Transcendence, Restoring the Spirit

Transitions

In life, we will experience transitions. The biggest transition we will make is from the physical form-based world to the transcendent, existential, spiritual realm. This chapter addresses the problem of change and transition to restore the spirit. Your faith can help you through these transitions and provide comfort when you are going through them. There are all kinds of transitions that we go through. As I write this chapter, my daughter is transitioning from middle school to high school. It is not just the grade change and a new school; it is the transition toward adulthood. I feel a bit depressed about it, I wish we had more time together. I am excited for her future but also a bit fearful about what her world will look like when I am not here. These are all normal fears that a parent has about their child as they age and grow up.

What transitions are you going through at this time?

What do you fear the most about the transition?

What do you need to move through the transition, and endure well?

In this chapter, we will explore what the shift toward awakened consciousness looks like. We will review some of the stories and teachings from the previous chapters and leave you with a clear path for restoring your sacred heart and purpose on this Earth.

The Roller Coaster

There are different ways people deal with change and transition. All are right, and all might be wrong depending on who you are and where you stand. One of the most useful models for understanding our emotions and spiritual wellness as we go through change is by Elizabeth Kubler Ross.[66] You might recognize this name from the five stages of grief literature and models that have been used by millions when experiencing grief and loss. She also developed the Roller Coast of Change to map what happens in the present and future with our emotions and soul as we move through change. We might begin with high expectations but then feel shocked, morning, guilt, loss, and need to let go. Once a decision is made, we might begin searching for new things and new answers; that might be why you bought this book. You were searching for answers to solve problems around spiritual emptiness and hopelessness. There are other emotions you will feel along the way, anger, fear, panic, loneliness, denial... and eventually, the tide will turn. You will find new relationships, new strengths and patterns, new ways of being in the world, and adjust to the loss that you have experienced.

If I wear my academic hat and begin thinking about my own losses, grief, and change, I see the truth. I know the Kubler-Ross cycle is accurate, at least for me. She outlines denial, anger, bargaining, depression, and acceptance as the five stages we go through when transitioning or grieving. Kubler-Ross created her work based on grief from the death of a loved one, but grief is also present in transitions. We grieve what we have lost, and we need time and resources to manage our emotions and tend to our spirits. We can appreciate and understand the word grief when we experience it. Grief can be suffering, loss, devastation, or change. I had no idea, for example, when I went through the divorce of my first husband, that I would grieve this relationship and loss for so long. Grief showed up in nearly every aspect of my being. I was angry, and I felt guilty. Looking back on this time,

I should have checked myself into serious therapy and rehabilitation. But I did not. I should have processed what was happening. It was the decisions that I made, and that we made, that led to the divorce. Life comes down to the choices that we make. We grieve more deeply when we notice that our choices have caused harm and suffering to others.

Animals become part of our psyche and lives, even more sometimes than humans we do life with. With my first relationship ending in divorce, it was not just the human I was grieving; it was our ten-year-old black lab, Daisy May. She would come to me in dreams. In some dreams, she was doing well, running through the fields; in others she was lost and looking for me. I woke up feeling torn and tortured. Lilly was our 14-year-old mutt we adopted in Montana. When she died, a piece of me died, at least, the physical part of our relationship died. Although she would still come to me in dreams, I would catch a glimpse of her out of the corner of my eye. At times I could smell her; she always smelled like cinnamon to me. Processing her transition was painful and deep. For anyone who has lost a beloved pet, you know the path that I am referring to. Getting over that took years.

Grandparents make the transition while many of us are young. My grandfather died when I was 19. He was the human here on Earth that was most like me, a friend and a mentor with tons of humor. He went to school until the 7th grade and started working on cars in the family junkyard. A few years later, he joined the army and was a mechanic in World War II placed at Hickam Field in Hawaii. I have lived a lot since he transitioned, but there are things that he taught me about being that are still with me today. His spirit was large; he laughed and made people feel welcome. He was humble because that was the only way he could be. He was poor by US standards in all things material, working as a parts counterman at the Big A Auto store in a rural Colorado town. But these material things did not matter much to me. I was in awe of how happy and content he was with the little that he had. He was rich in spirit but poor in all the things of this world that money could buy.

Friends and family will also transition while we live on Earth. A good friend passed away unexpectedly from an overdose. She struggled with addiction throughout her life. She was 46. It's been two years, and I am still grieving. There are no words for comfort or solitude in my grief. I have no comforting words to give her two teen children she left behind. A boyfriend I wanted to marry was tragically killed in a snowmobiling accident in the middle of the night. That same night I was dreaming of him- with a smile and twinkle in his eye, he told me that everything was going to be okay. About 10 minutes later I got the call from his best friend, he was gone.

I have been told that grief never goes away but our relationship with grief does. We begin to understand grief for what it is and see the love we have from our loved one who has passed away. Some believe that the spirits of our loved ones live in us.

Transitions

Transitions teach us where we are in the process of becoming awakened conscious spiritual beings. If we are in the first half of life, transitions can be so debilitating that we cannot manage life. Major life transitions where the physical form changes are windows into the second half of life and becoming consciousness, awakening. Many authors and gurus write about suffering and how suffering is the window toward spiritual growth and universal consciousness.[13,43] But no human really wants to suffer. Suffering can be physical and spiritual in nature, both leading to the same place. A place where we ask ourselves, "Is this all there is... there must be a purpose to the suffering."

Prisons are a place where suffering is happening and has happened. Many people end up in prison because they have made decisions while they were suffering that hurt other people. Consider the young man who was just 19 while driving under the influence and killed two innocent people walking across the street. He faces a lifetime in prison because of the temporary suffering he was experiencing and the manner in which he chose to cope with the suffering he was feeling. A relationship ended. Life in physical form was no longer what he dreamed it would be. The only option that he could think of was to drink to dull the pain that comes when relationships abruptly end. His story has been told a million times, about what happens when people make decisions that negatively impact others. But it is not all bad, prison, that is. Many people leave prison transformed, renewed, and awakened. They have found God in prison. They found hope; many earn college degrees, fight for justice, or sobriety...

Bryan Stevenson is an author, advocate, and visionary for social justice. His book, Just Mercy, changed how and what I think about justice in the US. He works to win legal challenges that include excessive and unfair sentencing. Bryan has exonerated death row prisoners and advocated for children who have been prosecuted as adults. His story, which is now a movie, Just Mercy, is the story of his life.[67] The teachings of his family, his vision for loving people, and his quest to make what is wrong right. The African Methodist Episcopal Church deeply influenced him as a child and young adult. Deep spiritual roots connected him to the segments of society that are unfair and unjust. His actions and the way that he lives demonstrate his deep love for Jesus and fellow human beings. When we sit with others in their suffering, we can make wrongs right.

Always do the right thing, even when the right this is the hard thing. - Brian Stevenson

There are four anchors of understanding social justice as a spiritual act:

Spirituality

Relationships

Values

Service and Action

Spirituality relates to practices, the essence of who you are without a form-based identity. Your identity in God or in the spiritual realm. Relationships reinforce our identities and values. Relationships can remind us of who we are beyond the physical, our unconsciousness. At the same time, we must be careful about getting attached to our physical identities, because they will change with time and space. When we are living out our values as spirituality guided beings, we can come from a space of helping service, empathy, kindness, and goodness. When we are in relationships that take away from our spirit, destroy our values, we experience stress and unease. It is up to you and me to be the model of awakening. What does this look like in your life? Spirituality is being able to call on a higher power and belief system when tragedy, trauma and things happen. When people can tap into their spirituality and beliefs in God, they have better results and outcomes in enduring well or transitioning.

Where is God in Transitions? God shows up in the little things that happen while we are in the midst of transitioning or watching our loved ones transition from the physical and form-based world to the spirit world. Death is the most obvious transition that people make from the form to the formless world. Here are other transitions that also prompt a spiritual awakening.

Near death experiences- sightings of God

Loss of loved ones- comfort from God

Voices and angels- cite stories

Strangers showing up- synchronicity

Words read or songs heard (on the radio or elsewhere)

In the kindness of others

The love for people

Forgiveness

The celebration

Many hold dear to the promises of the Bible and verses like John 14:3, "I go and will prepare a place for you..." Others believe that transitions are just part of life, and that when we die nothing happens. The secret in noticing God is being open and aware of the divine presence of him/her/it in our lives. Here God is not just a concept, the creator of the universe, or the maker of all things. God is awareness. God in us and outside of us. Fr. Richard Rohr's work on the Universal Christ is one way we experience God beyond the typical concepts of God.[68] Rohr reminds us that God loves things by becoming them. In this, God is in creation itself and in us, this is the ultimate evidence of awakening and consciousness.

Every time you choose love, you are in touch with the Divine Personality. You do not need to call it God. – Fr. Richard Rohr

This reminds me of the talks people have about God being real.... Usually, they go something like this. How do you know there is a God? I just do; it's in the Bible. Beyond the Bible, what signs have you seen of God? Look around, God is everywhere; it says in the Bible that God created the heavens and the Earth. Okay, well beyond that. Where is God, especially in suffering? God is aware of the suffering. Why does

God allow bad things to happen? Because of free will. When we suffer, God suffers too. This discussion can go back and forth for a long time. You can see that there is a difference here between the conceptual God found in the Bible, to the living God found in our hearts and minds and spiritual beings. Here awareness does not have words; it would be difficult to argue the point about God because it's a different way of knowing. It is based on a conscious awareness of a universal God, not a religion, dogma, orthodoxy, practice, or punishment. Language fails to adequately capture what God is, where God is, and why knowing and embodying God leads to awakened states of consciousness.

Friends to Call While in Jail

I've been traveling, seeing old friends who were once colleagues from the past. Many of them are getting older; they may not be here in the physical realm in the next year or two. I know this, and I feel it at a deep soul level. Linda is a Cheyenne Elder. We met about two decades ago on the Northern Cheyenne reservation. She was a wise old Indian woman, even at that time, and I was a young white researcher. I knew nothing and she must have sensed that because she offered me kindness in a cup of coffee and a toothless smile. It's the kind of kindness animals offer others in the wild when they sense that an animal is injured, elderly, or nearly dead, vulnerable in some way. Only I am not an animal. I am human, and she offered me pity and kindness that I gladly accepted and keep on accepting. Linda and I have been down many roads with projects, talks, people, drugs, kids, budgets, and more. She is someone I would call if I got locked up in jail, with just one chance to call someone. And I would not call her thinking that she would bail me out of jail because she's not a woman of any financial or material means. But I would call her because I would want her wisdom. I would want her to tell me that everything would be okay. She's seen more than I have, she's endured more, she's kind and gentle, she knows the path of hardship, and she is not afraid. She knows about things I could never know; I have not experienced them. Luckily, I am not locked up in jail, I am just sitting in the Salt Lake City airport, typing away on my MacBook trying to make sense of what it is about Linda that fills a void that I did not know I had. There are Lindas in the world if we stop to think about what it is about a person that completes us, fills a spiritual or knowing void that we cannot describe with words.

Think back on your life.

Who has offered you kindness like Linda?

What was in the kindness that made you know that it was genuine and real?

What was or is it about this person that made you feel comfortable, protected, and known?

Are you a Linda to other people? What would that look like?

Cultivating relationships that show empathy, kindness, respect, and deep knowing is a practice for restoring consciousness.

Evolving Worldviews

I know that I can write about Linda and the deep soul void that she fills because my worldview has shifted from that of a young white female researcher to a wiser one. Five years ago, Linda did not fill a spiritual void. She was not a human I would go to and seek comfort, guidance, care, or wisdom. I would have a cup of coffee with her, laugh, and even visit. But I would not hold her in this high regard, as a spiritual helper to me, as a human here to get me further down the path that I am meant to walk on.

I see in my life how the worldview prepares us for the shift, the shift from physical to spiritual and this occurs before we transition to the spiritual realm. Worldview also shifts us toward acceptance of what is. While some might say that all worldviews are obsessed with the conceptual form or the ego. I believe that worldviews are extremely helpful in making sense of our thoughts and why we think the way that we do. In Chapter 1, we reviewed worldviews and why they matter. We listed out various worldviews and what they look like in real-life so that you could easily match up your own views with a word or way of viewing what is. Worldviews are helpful because if you have landed at the end of this book and you feel without spirit or lacking a direction that is grounded in spiritual wellness, your worldview is influencing this.

> Do you see everything as a gift, or do you see everything as a burden to carry?

Worldviews are about our thinking. When you look at the world, is it loving and friendly? Or is it hateful, shameful, and scary? Whatever it is that you see, this is what you will keep getting and seeing until you change youth thoughts around what you see and experience. While our worldview is deeply influenced by our family, culture, and upbringing, there comes a time when we get to decide what the world is, what it looks like, and how we fit in. We can shed ideas, egos, teachings, and identities that are no longer helpful to us in our quest to become spiritually well, awakened, human souls. This does not require permission or approval from anyone or anything.

Going Deeper: I believe and know that when we drop our physical bodies, our spirits become part of a universal presence of God and love. I feel the presence of these spirits as I write this book. I cannot prove they are here helping me, but they are.

Loneliness and the True Self

A report by the US Surgeon General in May 2023 calls loneliness an epidemic.[7] Sources of loneliness are vast and deep and probably cannot be generalized. But we know that healthy relationships help us maintain our wellbeing, and this relational wellbeing can impact our spiritual wellbeing and connections. An 82-page report on loneliness calls for increased access to parks, public transportation, paid leave, and changes in the healthcare sector. And this is not surprising since research indicates that loneliness is not just a state of being, it contributes to heart disease, stroke, and dementia in older adults. And premature death in all populations. But the US Surgeon General and most of the people reading this report might be missing the cause. It is not about finding ways to connect people to tangible resources. It is about being aware of the true self, the spiritual self, that goes beyond the physical form- what we do, see, act, and feel.

> Think back to a time when you felt lonely.
>
> Were you physically alone?
>
> Were you spiritually alone?
>
> What emotions were you feeling? Anxious, depressed, disconnected?
>
> What did you do to feel connected, loved, and supported?

The beauty of awakening to spiritual wellbeing is that it takes away the physical dimension or at least lessens it. Meditation, prayer, and self-compassion are the path forward and can help. Even the most spiritually elevated mystics must remember to practice self-love and connect with their spirits to address loneliness.

He who knows others is learned. He who knows himself is wise. - Lao Tzu

Going Deeper: This conscious and intentional shift from a hateful to a friendly world, a gift-based world vs a burden-based world, matters. How we live is how we die. We are dying a physical death each day we live. But that which is real never dies. Our spirits do not die. They are not limited by time and Earthly existence.

Death

We all have the disease of death, and we are dying a physical death every day. Spiritual wellbeing helps us embrace this fact and walk toward physical death with less fear. Your thoughts about death are driven by your worldview and the stage of life you are in. People create internal narratives about the transition from form to formless, on Earth and in heaven. We will not fully know what happens when we die, until we die. Roughly seven-in-ten (72%) Americans say they believe in heaven — defined as a place "where people who have led good lives are eternally rewarded," according to the Pew Research Center's Religious Landscape Study. Consider these questions:

Are you in the first half or second half of your life?

Do you believe in heaven or hell?

Do you believe in nothing?

What part of you believes what it does?

But my Kingdom is not of this world. – Jesus of Nazareth

Anne is a religious woman. Every Sunday she attends church. There are no curse words in her vocabulary or using God's name in vain. Church is the gateway to heaven, and parishioners give her tips on how to live.

Anne's a Sunday school teacher, deacon, and on the mission committee. She holds many important positions and titles in the church. Reading the Bible every day, she is a walking audiobook of Bible history and verses. But she is physically dying, and I've been grieving this death since 2018 when she was diagnosed with a terminal and rare cancer. It's 2023, and death has not officially knocked at her door, but it's getting close. Last night we were at the emergency room. Eight weeks ago, she broke her back. She hasn't walked since then on her own. But we were there because she could not breathe, it was not the back that we were concerned about or even walking for that matter, it was the fact that air was not going in and out of her lungs like it should. Sitting and waiting in a claustrophobic room with a million places I would rather be, we had time to talk about a lot of things. One of the conversations related to transitions, from life to death, or the form to the formless. "Stop," she said. "I don't want to talk about death." She affirms she's a second-half of life person, but she is not comfortable with her own mortality. I told her it was okay to die. "No, stop," she demands. "We are not mentioning death anymore." When the time comes for her to leave the physical world, I think I will be more prepared than she is. Why is she afraid to die? If the Bible is true and heaven awaits, her beloved husband will be there greeting her at the pearly gates. Why then, is there so much fear in death?

When a man awakes, he awakes from the false assumption that he has always been awake, and therefore the master of his thoughts, feelings, and actions. – Henri Tracol

Awakening, a Never-Ending Process

There are days I am pitiful. I say things I do not mean. I act in ways that are not kind, loving, or God-like. I am full of ego, I think I am all-knowing, and I even say judgmental things. I could write a while about how unspiritual and unawakened and unconscious I am. I forget the Holy Spirit lives in me, and I am connected to God. I am helpful, generous, and loving - this is not me. God is acting through me. When I offer kindness or a smile to a stranger, this is not me. This is God in me. So, you can easily see how this goes; every offering of love comes from God. But if this is true, what about every bad thing you do? Does this come from God too? The choice comes from God. Consequence is an Earthly response to a choice that we make that does not fulfill our highest spiritual purpose. There are consequences to many Earthly choices and actions. Driving a car while drunk, killing someone. Cheating on a spouse, suffering a divorce. Or something more benign like lying about your weight on your driver's license and then having them recheck it when you board the small Alaska plane and having to look the gate agent in the eye and tell them you have gained 40 pounds since the photo. We create some of our own suffering here on Earth through the choices that we make. People suffer, even when they've made all the right choices. Two fourteen-year-olds were tragically killed in an accident last week. They made all the right choices. They still died and their families continue to suffer and grieve their tragic loss. A mother gives birth to a stillborn at the Billings Clinic. She's done everything right, took her vitamins, went to the prenatal visits, and Lamaze classes. Why did she have to suffer this loss? A child is diagnosed with terminal brain cancer, she dies just two months later. I do not believe we can know or fully explain why a loving God would allow these tragedies and suffering to happen. My elders tell me that there are some things we cannot understand or fully explain, they tell me this is part of The Great Mystery. I am not meant to make logical or even spiritual sense of these occurrences. This is disappointing, I appreciate clear, logical explanations. This is where faith comes in. God does not choose suffering for us, God is love. You are love. I am love. We are love.

People who've had any genuine spiritual experience always know that they don't know. They are utterly humbled before mystery. They are in awe before the abyss of it all, in wonder at eternity and depth, and a love, which is incomprehensible to the mind. - Fr. Richard Rohr

Transcendence and Healing the Spirit

We can rise above the egoic self, the pitiful and unkind shadow, the stranger to our best self when we awaken our consciousness. This begins with understanding that we are not our thoughts, our actions, our job title, our social identities, or our roles (as a teacher, mother, son, daughter, employee, etc.). I've transcended the ego in writing this book. My ego has rejected this book. Publishers have passed on it, with feedback that was not kind or constructive. These experiences gave me negative thoughts in my head and emotions that took me away from transcending the ego and a healed spirit. But I've landed here. My ego is behind me. It is a small barely visible spot on a wall. Part of the transcendence process is understanding that God can be called by many other names. That our spiritual awakening comes from our belief and love of God in us and in the world. We often get hung up on the names we give things like God, Creator, Divine, Master, Alah, She, Her, It, They. For a long time, I thought there was just one name, one path, but this process has demonstrated there are many. And if I am to follow the greatest teaching from the Bible, it is to Love God and Love others. Live out love. Love is the ethic that we live by. "Do justly, love mercy, walk justly," (Micah 6:8). I will hold onto these biblical teachings because they feel good, like a comfortable shoe I've been wearing for a while. It's the church camp I attended as an elementary school aged girl, lost and trying to find a place that my heart and spirit belongs to. I now see the home. The home for my spirit is knowing that God lives in me. Eckhart Tolle reminds me that I am the ocean, and my thoughts are just drops in the ocean. We are together riding the waves as one. This is the greatest teaching for me as I have written this book and tried to awaken my own consciousness rising.

Your consciousness is greater than your thoughts, your thoughts are drops in an ocean, and your consciousness is the ocean itself. Your ocean is a sum of all the thoughts which becomes your reality, learning to think clearly, presently and positively can revolutionize your existence. - Eckhart Tolle

My last book on spiritual healing[41] outlined anchors and ideas for transcending and healing the spirit. Read these to understand the awakening process. Awakening the spirit is not a destination. We do not walk on an awakened path and arrive at a destination. The destination is an inward journey or understanding, love, and connection. Awakening the spirit is not an outside job. There is nobody or no thing that can awaken you. Awakening comes from restoration of the mind, body, soul, and spirit. It's the balance that we strive for and the self-revelation, self-awareness, self-acknowledgement, self-understanding that comes. We look to pills, people, books, therapy, and more. These might help us, but they alone will not heal and transcend us. Awakening consciousness involves service, generosity, forgiveness, and love. When we see acts of service, generosity, and love, we see and feel awakening in our lives and the lives of people on similar paths. We can recognize the path because we are on that path too. Awakening is a healing of our spirits, a journey. When we embrace spiritual practices, service to others, and uplifting beliefs, we find other people who are on similar paths. There is reassurance in being with others who embrace the Great Mystery and endure well. In this book, we have been on a journey and explored the spiritual dimensions of being and what consciousness rising looks like. We have considered topics like worldview, identity, suffering, evidence, and spiritual dimensions of wellness. In each chapter, we read stories of the spiritually well or those who have lived in a way that encompasses the spiritual dimensions of wellbeing. Most of this is subjective; there is flexibility that is required because there are no two spirits that are identical. This is one of the major challenges of organized religion—our spirits are not the same. We all have our own ideas about what these dimensions should look like in our own lives. As you finish this book, there are a few words I want to leave you with.

Heal. We do not need to be a spiritual guru, pastor, monk, or physical to heal. Remember, to heal just means positive change. We can and do know things about our spiritual wellbeing because of how we live and our status as conscious, awakened, spiritual, connected, sacred, humans.

Find your true self, your spirit. Many are in a spiritual crisis right now. They lack purpose, and this shows up in all kinds of ways. If you are not sure where you are on the spiritual wellness continuum, consider first, how you spend your time.

What do you value?

What do you give meaning to?

How do you find purpose in living a physical existence?

Answers to these questions are as deep as the Pacific Ocean and as wide as the gate to heaven.

We become what we think. Be aware of your subconscious mind.

What stories are you telling yourself every day about who you are and where you are going?

Consider creating new stories about what you want your future to be. Many have tested this practice, and it works. Why not give it a try?

Acknowledge you are a spirit living in a physical body. If we fail to acknowledge our spiritual existence, we will live a lonely, shallow, and disconnected life. Do not wait until bad things happen, transitions occur, and suffering shows up to begin walking on a spiritual path.

Going Deeper: Our future and ability to rise as awakened conscious humans is based on our connection to God (called by many other names). Remember that God is most concerned about being and not doing. Thoughts take us away from being. Observe your thoughts.

The door is wide open. It is inviting you in. Every human on this planet and beyond has the capacity to become an awakened, conscious, enlightened, aware, and balanced spiritual being who gives love and is love to others. Consciousness rising is about bringing you into the sacred circle and dance of what we call living here on Earth.

Final Takeaway: You ultimately get to decide how much you will love in this life. You decide what your life here on Earth looks like. You choose how to walk on a narrow path that will take you home to your enduring and unending spiritual nature and being. Choice is the practice of your one sacred identity.

Resources

Bryan Stevenson, Equal Justice Initiative. https://eji.org/bryan-stevenson/

Eckhart Tolle, Stillness Speaks, https://eckharttolle.com/stillness-speaks-excerpt/

The Psychology of Mattering, https://www.sciencedirect.com/book/9780128094150/the-psychology-of-mattering

Reflections for Going Deeper

Read. What did you read that speaks to your true self, your sacred identity?

Reflect. How will you live your life? What choices will you make?

Remember. What can you remember that will help you awaken your consciousness?

Abide. What do you accept as a practice to restore and recalibrate your consciousness?

References

1. Nobriga, A. (Host) (2024). Healing and Human Potential Podcast. The 4 Stages of Spiritual Awakening + Secrets to Manifestation with Michael Beckwith. [Audio podcast]. YouTube. https://www.youtube.com/watch?v=c_iag_vvbdM

2. Greenwood, S. (2022). Black Americans Have a Clear Vision for Reducing Racism, but Little Hope It Will Happen. Pew Research Center Race & Ethnicity. Published August 30, 2022. https://www.pewresearch.org/race-ethnicity/2022/08/30/black-americans-have-a-clear-vision-for-reducing-racism-but-little-hope-it-will-happen/

3. National Sexual Violence Resource Center. (2023). National Sexual Violence Resource Center. https://www.nsvrc.org/statistics

4. Centers for Disease Control and Prevention. (2023). Data Overview: Opioids. https://www.cdc.gov/opioids/data/index.html

5. Centers for Disease Control and Prevention. (2023). Suicide Data and Statistics. https://www.cdc.gov/suicide/suicide-data-statistics.html

6. Beech, B, Ford, C., Thorpe, R., Bruce, M., Norris, K. (2021). Poverty, Racism, and the Public Health Crisis in America. Front Public Health. 2021; 9:699049. doi:10.3389/fpubh.2021.699049

7. United States Health and Human Services (2023). New Surgeon General Advisory Raises Alarm about the Devastating Impact of the Epidemic of Loneliness and Isolation in the United States. https://www.hhs.gov/about/news/2023/05/03/new-surgeon-general-advisory-raises-alarm-about-devastating-impact-epidemic-loneliness-isolation-united-states.html

8. Pew Research Center. (2019). In the U.S., the Decline of Christianity Continues at Rapid Pace, an update on America's changing religious landscape. https://www.pewresearch.org/religion/2019/10/17/in-u-s-decline-of-christianity-continues-at-rapid-pace/

9. Friedman, P. (2018) Life Balance, Emotional Stability, Well-Being, and Spiritual Awakening. International Journal of Healing and Caring, Volume 18, No. 1, 1-22.

10. U.S.A. Facts (2023). Population by year, race, age, ethnicity, & more. USA Facts. https://usafacts.org/data/topics/people-society/population-and-demographics/our-changing-population/

11. U.S. Census (2021). 2020 Census Illuminates Racial and Ethnic Composition of the Country. https://www.census.gov/library/stories/2021/08/improved-race-ethnicity-measures-reveal-united-states-population-much-more-multiracial.html

12. Johnson, V. & Carter, R. (2020). Black Cultural Strengths and Psychosocial Well-Being: An Empirical Analysis With Black American Adults. J Black Psychol. 46(1):55-89. doi:10.1177/0095798419889752

13. Reyes-Ortiz, C., Rodriguez, M., Markides, K. (2009). The Role of Spirituality Healing with Perceptions of the Medical Encounter among Latinos. J Gen Intern Med. 24(Suppl 3):542-547. doi:10.1007/s11606-009-1067-9

14. Statista. (2022). Sexual orientation and gender identity U.S. by generation 2021. Statista. https://www.statista.com/statistics/1331358/sexual-orientation-gender-identity-us/

15. Wright, A, & Stern, S. (2016). The role of spirituality in sexual minority identity. Psychology of Sexual Orientation and Gender Diversity, 3(1), 71.

16. Rohr, R. (2012). Gender, God And Spirituality. Huffington Post. https://www.huffpost.com/entry/gender-god-and-spirituality_b_1624932

17. Statista (2021). Disability in the U.S. Statista. https://www.statista.com/topics/4380/disability-in-the-us/

18. Hodge, D., & Reynolds, C. (2019). Spirituality among people with disabilities: A nationally representative study of spiritual and religious profiles. Health & Social Work, 44(2), 75-86.

19. Mitchell, T. (2021). About Three-in-Ten U.S. Adults Are Now Religiously Unaffiliated. Pew Research Center's Religion & Public Life Project. https://www.pewresearch.org/religion/2021/12/14/about-three-in-ten-u-s-adults-are-now-religiously-unaffiliated/

20. Greenwood, S. (2021). Views About National Identity Becoming More Inclusive in U.S., Western Europe. Pew Research Center's Global Attitudes Project. https://www.pewresearch.org/global/2021/05/05/views-about-national-identity-becoming-more-inclusive-in-us-western-europe/

21. Mulukom, V. (2020). How non-religious worldviews provide solace in times of crisis. The Conversation. http://theconversation.com/how-non-religious-worldviews-provide-solace-in-times-of-crisis-138638

22. Flett, G. (2018). The psychology of mattering: Understanding the human need to be significant. Academic Press. 345.

23. Rosenberg, M., & McCullough, B. (1981). Mattering: Inferred Significance and Mental Health among Adolescents. Research in Community Mental Health, 2, 163-182.

24. Bitsko, R. (2022). Mental health surveillance among children—United States, 2013–2019. MMWR supplements, 71.

25. Foley, L., Krengel, S., Rutzick, S., & Waller, C. (2022). Recommendations for a Proposed Hennepin County Guaranteed Basic Income Pilot Program. University Minnesota.

26. Centers for Disease Control and Prevention. (2022). Obesity is a Common, Serious, and Costly Disease. Obesity and Socioeconomic Status. https://www.cdc.gov/obesity/data/adult.html

27. Reeves, R., Adams, C., Dubbert, P., Hickson, D., & Wyatt, S. (2012). Are religiosity and spirituality associated with obesity among African Americans in the Southeastern United States (the Jackson Heart Study)? Journal of religion and health, 51, 32-48.

28. Hu, K., & Staiano, A. (2022). Trends in obesity prevalence among children and adolescents aged 2 to 19 years in the US from 2011 to 2020. JAMA pediatrics, 176(10), 1037-1039.

29. Caner, N., Efe, Y., & Başdaş, Ö. (2022). The contribution of social media addiction to adolescent LIFE: Social appearance anxiety. Current Psychology, 41(12), 8424-8433.

30. Centers for Disease Control and Prevention (2023). Disability Impacts All of Us Infographic. https://www.cdc.gov/ncbddd/disabilityandhealth/ infographic-disability-impacts-all.html

31. Peter G Peterson Foundation. (2023, September 25). 7 Key Trends in Poverty in the United States. https://www.pgpf.org/blog/2023/02/7-key-trends-in-poverty-in-the-united-states

32. Chopra, D., & Platt-Finger, S. (2023). Living in the Light: Yoga for Self-realization. Harmony.

33. Hamilton, J. (2022). In jumpy flies and fiery mice, scientists see the roots of human emotions. National Public Radio. https://www.npr.org/sections/health-shots/2022/ 04/06/1091086672/animal-human-emotions

34. Anderson, D. (2022). The nature of the beast: how emotions guide us. Basic Books.

35. Harker, L., & Keltner, D. (2001). Expressions of positive emotion in women's college yearbook pictures and their relationship to personality and life outcomes across adulthood. Journal of personality and social psychology, 80(1), 112.

36. Prochaska, J., & DiClemente, C. (1983). Stages and processes of self-change of smoking: toward an integrative model of change. Journal of consulting and clinical psychology, 51(3), 390.

37. Alexander, E. (2012). Proof of heaven: A neurosurgeon's journey into the afterlife. Simon and Schuster.

38. Melore, C. (2021). Paranormal nation: Two-thirds of Americans believe in ghosts or aliens. https://studyfinds.org/americans-believe-ghosts-aliens-paranormal/

39. Paloutzian, R., & Ellison, C. (1982). Spiritual well-being scale. A spiritual strategy for counseling and psychotherapy.

40. Bansal, A., & Sharma, S. (2003). Can spiritual health be quantified: A simple idea. Abstract. In International Conference on Statistics, Combinatorics, and related areas. University of Southern Maine. Portland, ME, USA (pp. 3-5).

41. Bożek, A., Nowak, P., & Blukacz, M. (2020). The relationship between spirituality, health-related behavior,

and psychological well-being. Frontiers in Psychology, 11, 1997.

42. Oman, D. (2018). Reviewing religion/spirituality evidence from a public health perspective: Introduction. Why religion and spirituality matter for public health: Evidence, implications, and resources, 19-26.

43. Puchalski, C. (2001, October). The role of spirituality in health care. In Baylor University Medical Center Proceedings (Vol. 14, No. 4, pp. 352-357). Taylor & Francis.

44. Kelley, A. (2022) Treatment Program Evaluation: Public Health Perspectives on Mental Health and Substance Use Disorders. Vol 1. Routledge.

45. Dickerson, D. , Venner, K. , Duran, B., Annon, J., Hale, B., & Funmaker, G. (2014). Drum-Assisted Recovery Therapy for Native Americans (DARTNA): Results from a pretest and focus groups. American Indian and Alaska native mental health research (Online), 21(1), 35.

46. Kabat-Zinn, J. (2015). Mindfulness. Mindfulness, 6(6), 1481-1483.

47. Garland, E., Manusov, E., Froeliger, B., Kelly, A., Williams, J., & Howard, M. (2014). Mindfulness-oriented recovery enhancement for chronic pain and prescription opioid misuse: results from an early-stage randomized controlled trial. Journal of consulting and clinical psychology, 82(3), 448.

48. Bear, R., Choate, P., & Lindstrom, G. (2022). Theoretical research: Reconsidering Maslow and the

hierarchy of needs from a First Nations perspective. Aotearoa New Zealand Social Work, 34(2), 30-41.

49. Helliwell, J. (2023). World Happiness Trust and Social Connections in Times of Crisis. https://worldhappiness.report/ed/2023/world-happiness-trust-and-social-connections-in-times-of-crisis/

50. Compton, W., & Hoffman, E. (2019). Positive psychology: The science of happiness and flourishing. Sage Publications.

51. Knight, Z. (2017). A proposed model of psychodynamic psychotherapy linked to Erik Erikson's eight stages of psychosocial development. Clinical psychology & psychotherapy, 24(5), 1047-1058.

52. Kelley, A. & BigFoot, D. (2024). Spiritual Healing from Trauma and Addiction: Discussions of Mental Health, Recovery, and Faith. Routledge, Taylor, and Francis Group.

53. Cox, D. (2022). Generation Z and the Future of Faith in America. Survey Center on American Life. https://www.americansurveycenter.org/research/generation-z-future-of-faith/

54. Kelley, A, Bingham, D, Brown, E, Pepion, L. (2017). Assessing the Impact of American Indian Peer Recovery Support on Substance Use and Health. J Groups Addict Recovery. 2017;12(4):296-308.

55. Duran, E. (2006). Healing the Soul Wound: Counseling with American Indians and Other Native Peoples. Teachers

College Press. http://catdir.loc.gov/catdir/toc/fy0609/2005046666.html

56. Kelley, A, Giroux, J, Schulz, M, et al. (2014). American Indian diabetes mortality in the Great Plains Region 2002-2010. BMJ Open Diabetes Res Care. 2015;3(1).

57. American Diabetes Association. (2023) Statistics About Diabetes. https://diabetes.org/about-diabetes/statistics

58. Moore, D. & Coyhis, D. (2010) The Multicultural Wellbriety Peer Recovery Support Program: Two Decades of Community-Based Recovery. Alcohol Treat Q. 28(3):273-292.

59. Katerndahl, D. (2008). Impact of Spiritual Symptoms and Their Interactions on Health Services and Life Satisfaction. Ann Fam Med. 6(5):412-420.

60. Simard, S. (2021). Finding the mother tree: Uncovering the wisdom and intelligence of the forest. Penguin U.K.

61. Brooks, D. (2020). The second mountain: The quest for a moral life. Random House Trade Paperbacks.

62. Hynd S. (2021). Trauma, Violence, and Memory in African Child Soldier Memoirs. Culture, medicine, and psychiatry, 45(1), 74–96.

63. Shepard, M. F., & Pence, E. L. (Eds.). (1999). Coordinating community responses to domestic violence: Lessons from Duluth and beyond. Sage Publications.

64. Breen, W. E., Kashdan, T. B., Lenser, M. L., & Fincham, F. D. (2010). Gratitude and forgiveness: Convergence and divergence on self-report and informant ratings. Personality and individual differences, 49(8), 932-937.

65. Watkins, P., Woodward, K., Stone, T., & Kolts, R. (2003). Gratitude and happiness: Development of a measure of gratitude and relationships with subjective well-being. Social Behavior and Personality: an international journal, 31(5), 431-451.

66. Kubler-Ross, E., & Kessler, D. (2005). On grief and grieving: Finding the meaning of grief through the five stages of loss. Simon and Schuster.

67. Stevenson, B. (2019). Just Mercy (movie tie-in edition): A story of justice and redemption. One World.

68. Griswold, E. (2020). Richard Rohr Reorders the Universe. New Yorker. https://www.newyorker.com/news/on-religion/richard-rohr-reorders-the-universe

69. Pew Research Center (2015). America's Changing Religious Landscape. https://www.pewresearch.org/religion/2015/05/12/americas-changing-religious-landscape/

ABOUT THE AUTHOR

Allyson Kelley is an author, researcher, professor, mother and person who remembers. She writes about research, teaching, wellness, and healing. Her work has been featured in several journals including the American Psychological Association, Journal of American Medical Association, Lancet, American Journal of Public Health, and numerous other outlets. Allyson finds peace and God in the outdoors, and sometimes a Sunday sermon. She is living her best life in the mountains of Central Oregon.

Don't miss out!

Visit the website below and you can sign up to receive emails whenever Allyson Kelley publishes a new book. There's no charge and no obligation.

https://books2read.com/r/B-A-SDZGB-ZLIFF

BOOKS 2 READ

Connecting independent readers to independent writers.

About the Publisher

AKA Published is an independent press committed to producing high-quality books and resources that transform, connect, and heal.

Read more at akapublished.com.

www.ingramcontent.com/pod-product-compliance
Lightning Source LLC
Chambersburg PA
CBHW051239130726
47988CB00001B/409